CHRISTMAS
EXPOSED

Library of Congress Cataloging in Publication Number: 2011922701

ISBN: 978-1-59474-542-3

Printed in China

Typeset in Cheltenham, Franklin Gothic, Trade Gothic, and Utopia

Designed by Katie Hatz
Production management by John J. McGurk

Quirk Books
215 Church Street
Philadelphia, PA 19106
quirkbooks.com

10 9 8 7 6 5 4 3 2 1

the ONION PRESENTS

CHRISTMAS

HOLIDAY COVERAGE FROM AMERICA'S FINEST NEWS SOURCE

by the Staff of
the ONION

QUIRK BOOKS
PHILADELPHIA

Sales Manager Gets A Little Crazy At Office Party

SUNNYVALE, CA–Allen Wohl, a 33-year-old associate sales manager at M&H Marketing, got a little crazy at Tuesday's annual office holiday party, held from 2 to 3 p.m. in the third-floor conference room.

The combination Christmas and New Year's party, thrown in November to avoid conflicting with M&H Marketing's traditional December busy season, was highlighted by Wohl's irreverent antics, which included silly faces, impersonations of co-workers and humorous poses atop a desk.

"Allen has always been known as M&H's resident cut-up, but he really cut loose at the party," promotions coordinator Janice Larkspahr said. "At one point, he made a bullhorn out of a paper plate and sang the *Gilligan's Island* theme song, only he changed the lyrics to be about people in our office. You don't even want to know what he said about [senior sales manager] Richard [Stenstrup]."

"That Allen Wohl is one certified nutball," secretary Irene Utter said. "When he picked up that tray of punch cups and pretended to be a British waiter, I almost died laughing. Where does he come up with that stuff?"

Asked for comment on the incident, Wohl said, "What can I say? I'm a wild and crazy guy!"

Sales manager Allen Wohl, whose zany behavior at a recent holiday office party was described by fellow M&H Marketing employees as "certifiable."

The highlight of the party, most members of the M&H Marketing team agreed, came when Wohl presented "awards" to his co-workers.

"My certificate said 'Most Likely To Leave The Presentation On The Plane,'" said sales supervisor Randall Talish, who last December left a proposal for a $26,000 Tru-Bilt Windows & Siding ad campaign on a flight from Los Angeles. "I've got to admit, he really got me good with that one. I was hoping everyone had forgotten about that goof-up by now, but leave it to Allen to give me heck."

The hour-long party, which also featured cake, soda, festive yellow streamers and a rousing game of Scattergories, was deemed a success by all.

"I was having so much fun, I almost didn't want to go back to work," associate marketing supervisor Sheila Duckett said. "Allen sure was in rare form."

Those who work closely with Wohl said the behavior was typical of the man they call "M&H's answer to Jay Leno."

> ### "'At one point, he made a bullhorn out of a paper plate and sang the *Gilligan's Island* theme song, only he changed the lyrics to be about people in our office. You don't even want to know what he said about Richard."

"Allen's a real prankster," fellow sales manager Gene Budzig said. "I remember that one time last month, when Bill McCullers was saying all morning that he had to make sure to FedEx a proposal that day, but when he went to drop off the package, Wohl told him the FedEx guy had just left. You should've seen the look on Bill's face when Allen told him he was just kidding! Boy, was he relieved!"

In addition to playing pranks on co-workers, Wohl expresses his unorthodox personality by decorating his cubicle in an offbeat manner. Adorning his workspace is a Far Side mousepad, an Executive Stress-Relief Koosh Ball, novelty windshield-wiper sunglasses, a Dilbert screen-saver, and a framed sign that reads, "There Is No 'I' In 'Team'... But Fortunately, There Is One In 'Vacation'!"

Wohl also has an arsenal of humorous quips he has used throughout his seven years with M&H Marketing, including, "Time to make the donuts," which he proclaims upon arriving at work each morning, and "Cha-ching!" which he shouts after closing a deal with a new client.

Though M&H employees settled down and returned to their normal work routines shortly after the party, a resurgence in excitement over it is expected Friday, when office manager Jan Schenkle will get her roll of pictures back from Walgreen's. Schenkle, who is in charge of compiling the office newsletter, said she plans to display the photos on the break-room bulletin board.

"When those pictures come back, Allen is going to hear about his crazy shenanigans from everybody all over again," Schenkle said. "I just hope we got a good shot of him balancing that plate of cake on his head."

Wohl said he enjoys all the attention.

"I've always loved the spotlight," he said. "It's a real kick to be able to make your co-workers laugh. Of course, I can't be a card all the time, or our department's productivity would take a major hit. Still, it's nice to go off the deep end every once in a while." ∅

NEWS IN PHOTOS

Pet Winterized

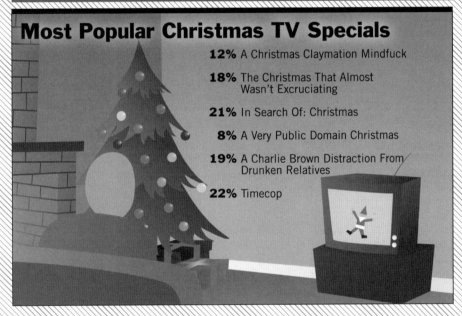

Most Popular Christmas TV Specials

12% A Christmas Claymation Mindfuck

18% The Christmas That Almost Wasn't Excruciating

21% In Search Of: Christmas

8% A Very Public Domain Christmas

19% A Charlie Brown Distraction From Drunken Relatives

22% Timecop

Emotionally Distant Family Spends Holidays Watching Touching Family Dramas Together

RUTLAND, VT—In what has become an annual holiday tradition, the dysfunctional Dawes family came together Sunday to sit in front of the TV and watch touching, feel-good family dramas in stony silence.

The Dawes grimly watch *It's A Wonderful Life*.

"We see each other so rarely," said Nicole Dawes, 44, whose three children were all home from college. "It's so nice to all sit down together and have a peaceful time. And [son] Kevin didn't bring up that awful new girlfriend of his once the entire time."

Following a special holiday dinner of turkey, artichokes, and spiced yams, Nicole and sullen daughter Gabrielle, an 18-year-old freshman at the University of Vermont, were put in charge of selecting the movies to watch. The two shared a wordless 10-minute car trip to their local Blockbuster video store, where Gabrielle ruled out most of her mother's choices as "stupid" or "lame." Tired of saying no and eager to leave the store, Gabrielle finally assented to the holiday classic *It's A Wonderful Life* and the 1994 remake of *Miracle On 34th Street*.

"I can't believe we got *Miracle On 34th Street* again," Gabrielle said. "Still, it's better than some of the other stuff my mom was pulling off the shelves. I mean, *The Santa Clause*? How gay is that? I hate Tim Allen."

Added Gabrielle: "I wish we hadn't gotten *It's A Wonderful Life*. It's so long. Besides, why would anybody pay actual money to rent that thing when it's on TV, like, a bazillion times every December?"

> **"'I can't believe we got *Miracle On 34th Street* again. Still, it's better than some of the other stuff my mom was pulling off the shelves. I mean, *The Santa Clause*? How gay is that? I hate Tim Allen.'"**

Upon Nicole and Gabrielle's return, *It's A Wonderful Life* was promptly inserted into the living-room VCR. Familiar with the annual routine, the family members huddled around the TV without exchanging a word, just as they have since the holiday tradition began in 1991.

As the movie played, Kevin, 22, a senior at Southern Vermont College, paid little attention, wrapped up in thoughts of his impending graduation. The few times he did focus on the film, it was to negatively compare his own family to the Baileys.

"That movie always makes me think about how if dad's hardware store lost $8,000 like George Bailey's bank did, it'd totally tear us apart," Kevin said. "He'd probably blame us and drag us all down with him. Good thing he isn't trusted with much money at his job."

Following the conclusion of *It's A Wonderful Life*, an awkward 80-second silence occurred as the videotape rewound. The silence was briefly broken by daughter Gina, 20, who remarked that the evening's dinner had been "really good." Peter, her father, grunted in agreement.

As *Miracle On 34th Street* played, Peter sat in rapt attention, pushing aside anxieties about work, aging, and his chilly relationship with his children.

"The original was one of my all-time favorites," Peter said. "I was trying to spot the differences between the two. I was just glad to have something to focus on besides trying to make conversation with the kids. I have no idea what they're up to these days. Jesus, they're all grown up, able to vote and all. I wonder if they hate me."

Some 40 minutes into the movie, having consumed three snifters of brandy, Peter fell asleep.

When the second movie finished, the three children claimed exhaustion and trundled off to their childhood bedrooms, feigning excitement for the following day's Christmas-tree-shopping excursion.

> **"'I was just glad to have something to focus on besides trying to make conversation with the kids. I have no idea what they're up to these days. Jesus, they're all grown up, able to vote and all. I wonder if they hate me.'"**

"It's good to see all the kids together under one roof. It reminds me of when they would all watch cartoons together growing up," said Nicole, wiping a tear from her eye. "I love the holidays." *Ø*

Company To Get Head Start On Christmas Layoffs This Year

OAK BROOK, IL—Confirming their intention not to wait until the last minute the way they usually do, executives at Visatex Inc. said Friday they planned to get an early start on this year's Christmas layoffs. "I'm always so busy that I've been getting to our layoff list later and later each holiday season," said CEO Thomas Barnaby, adding that some of his more organized executive friends get all their terminations out of the way by Thanksgiving. "Last year we got so backed up that a few people didn't find out they were getting let go until Christmas Eve." Company officials added that they hoped the head start would give them a chance to actually relax and enjoy the holidays for once.

It'll Be A Blue Christmas Without Stuff

You know that old Christmas carol that goes, "Christmas is coming, the goose is getting fat, please put a penny in the old man's hat"? Well, might I suggest a slight lyric change to "please put a penny in Jean Teasdale's hat"? And, instead of "a penny," make it "$2,756.29"? Because that's how much my Visa bill is right now, and I'm afraid that Christmas at the Teasdales is not going to be too merry this year if I don't find a way to pay this thing off pronto!

A Room Of Jean's Own
By Jean Teasdale

It's not like I haven't been trying to pay it off. I mean, I've been working my tail off at Fashion Bug. (I'm up to 30 hours a week!) I'd work even more if my boss, Roz, would let me, but she hired a new girl, Ellen, who wanted extra hours, too. That irked me a little. After all, it's not like we get a huge amount of business anyway, especially on weekdays, and having an extra person around seems kind of unnecessary. But Ellen is a friend of Roz's, so that got her an automatic in at the Bug. Plus, she's always going off about how she's a single mom with two kids and is strapped for cash. Don't get me wrong: I love kids to pieces and hope to have some of my own someday. (Can't you hear those loud ticks coming from my biological clock?) But just because Ellen is a mom, that doesn't make her better than me. We all have crosses to bear. I mean, I've got a police record now, but you don't hear me trying to get sympathy or favoritism from it.

It's a shame that I'm in such debt, because my own X-mas wish list is about a mile long this year. And, after the Year From Hell that I had, I deserve a little something nice! Of course, I've got one thing going for me, the fact that my family is no longer speaking to me due to that little born-again Christian fiasco of mine. So at least I'll save a few hundred bucks not buying presents for them!

Also on the plus side, hubby Rick agreed to pay the entire amount of rent until I have my debts paid off! The only catch is, he made me promise to pay for the groceries, utilities, car insurance, and cable, not to mention settle at least half my credit-card debt before I even thought of splurging on myself at the mall. The fact that I couldn't get more hours at Fashion Bug didn't soften him a bit. "Just get a second job," he snorted. (Sheesh! Heil Hubby!)

> "Just because Ellen is a mom, that doesn't make her better than me. I mean, I've got a police record now, but you don't hear me trying to get sympathy or favoritism from it."

Still, I can't stop dreaming about the stuff I'd love to buy myself this X-mas. For example, I just know there's a DVD player out there with my name on it. Have you seen these things? They're amazing! They can squeeze an entire movie onto a single CD!

I swear, after seeing one at Best Buy the other day, I wanted to go straight home and throw our VCR in the garbage! The only thing better than a DVD player would be a DVD player with a Patrick Swayze movie in it all cued up and ready to go! (Rowrr, rowrr!)

"Well, I may have had a lot of Grinches to contend with this year, but that doesn't mean I've lost my belief in Santa Claus!"

There's also a great T-shirt I saw at Spencer Gifts. It says, "I'm A Shopaholic In A 12-Step Program. Steps 1 Through 11: Shop. Step 12: Get Drunk After You See Your Credit-Card Bill." My God, whoever came up with that shirt must be a regular reader of my column! Anyway, I've just got to have that thing!

Now, you Jeanketeers out there know that I have a terminal case of Precious Momentsitis, and there's a figurine I'm just dying for. It's a little girl who's about to set a dessert in her heart-shaped cupboard, only to find a darling kitten in it! It's called—what else?—"You Have A Special Place In My Heart." Well, that figurine sure has a special place in mine! (Only problem is, it would also have a special place in my wallet... to the tune of $55!)

I'm also constantly seeing things I want in the dozens of catalogs I get in the mail each month. I really like those miniature indoor water fountains they sell now. They're supposed to alleviate stress and relax you. And, seeing how hectic my life has been lately, I could really use one! I was trying to persuade hubby Rick to buy one since he's always so uptight, but he just said, "They look Oriental. They're probably Chinese water-torture machines designed to drive Americans insane." (Boy, way to prove my point, Rick!)

Okay, okay, I admit it. I have champagne tastes. Jean Teasdale always wants nothing but the best. As my mother, from whom I am now estranged, likes to say, "The moment Jean has a dollar in her pocket, she'll find a way to spend it!" Well, I may have had a lot of Grinches to contend with this year, but that doesn't mean I've lost my belief in Santa Claus!

I don't often admit this to people, but I still believe in Santa Claus. Not in him literally existing, but in the belief that the holidays are a time for magic, and that people will get rewarded for trying their best. Call me an incurable optimist, but it does happen. In fact, it just happened to me. This morning, I was taking my winter coat out of storage and, upon reaching into the pocket, I pulled out a real sight for sore eyes: a $20 bill! And this is one $20 bill that Grinch Rick and his austerity plan will never get, because I'm going out right now and buying one of those hilarious singing bass. They've been out for months now and, darn it, I deserve one!

Oh, don't worry: Rick is on my shopping list, too. After all, 'tis better to give than to receive, right? Only, I don't think he should get one of those inflatable NFL chairs he wants so much. No, I think a gift-wrapped cinnabar candle from Fashion Bug will do just fine. They're 50 percent off right now, and with my employee discount, it'll cost practically nothing. Rick will be proud of my frugality, I'm sure!

(Ain't I a stinker?!?) ✍

Not Snowing Over Here, Man On Phone Reports

DES MOINES, IA—During a brief, five-minute telephone conversation last Monday, local resident Grant Jacobs, 58, reportedly expressed surprise that it was not snowing near his home in Des Moines, IA, even though it was snowing in Providence, RI, where his son Michael, 20, attends college. "It's actually pretty clear, here," Jacobs said. "I bet you guys are getting what we had last week." Jacobs added that, according to the Weather Channel's Doppler radar, the weather should be fine in Providence tomorrow, while Des Moines is supposed to get hit pretty hard.

Jesus 'Really Dreading' This Next Birthday

JERUSALEM—Jesus Christ, son of God and savior of humanity, confided Monday that He is not looking forward to His 2,000th birthday next year, saying that He is "really dreading turning the big two-oh-oh-oh."

Christ anxiously eyes his fast-approaching birthday.

"This is the Big One," said Christ, who will be 1,999 Dec. 25. "I can't believe I'm actually turning 2,000 soon. I am seriously getting up there."

Though His associates have been keeping Him in good company as the milestone draws near, Christ said He is finding it increasingly difficult to keep His spirits up.

"They keep telling me I don't look a day over 33, but you know how they are—especially Peter," Christ said meekly. "He'll be calling me an old fogy three times before the cock crows tomorrow morning. I just know it."

Even members of Christ's family have been giving Him a hard time about His age.

"Dad's been ribbing Me pretty good," said Christ, sipping Holy Water from an "Old Fart" mug recently given to Him by St. Michael. "He gives Me all kinds of grief, telling Me stuff like, 'At the rate you're going, people aren't going to know if you're the son of God or the brother.'"

"Two thousand," Christ said. "I swear, for the next few centuries, when people ask me how old I am, I'm going to tell them 1,999."

Though Christ is aware that His birthday is one of Earth's biggest holidays, He said it hasn't been important to Him lately.

> **"'They keep telling me I don't look a day over 33, but you know how they are—especially Peter. He'll be calling me an old fogy three times before the cock crows tomorrow morning. I just know it.'"**

"I remember when I turned 1,000, I was really excited," said Christ. "A bunch of the apostles threw a big surprise party for me at the Sea of Galilee, and it was such a great time—I don't even want to tell you how much water we turned into wine that night. But once I turned 1,000, each birthday sort of became less and less of a big deal. It's like, once you're a thousandsomething, you don't even get so excited about birthdays anymore. The past few hundred birthdays, I've generally celebrated by just going out to dinner with a good friend or something mellow like that."

"I am so over the hill," He said. "God, in another 501 years, I'm going to be 2,500. I can't believe it."

Despite Christ's pleading with friends

not to "make a whole big production" out of His birthday, some suspect He is secretly hoping for a surprise party.

> ## "'It was such a great time—I don't even want to tell you how much water we turned into wine that night.'"

"Every time I bring up the subject, He says, 'Don't do anything special for Me, don't get me any presents, all I want is peace on Earth, I'm not some kid in his 840s anymore'—blah, blah, blah," St. Matthew said. "That's vintage Jesus for you. Well, I have news for Him: Nobody is going to 'just forget.'"

Still, Christ insisted that He hopes no big celebrations are in the works.

"It's bad enough getting old, but having your birthday on Christmas?" said Christ, shaking His head. "And Dad had better not make one of those delicious carrot cakes

A photo of Jesus Christ celebrating his 1,998th birthday at a small, informal party

with the sour-cream frosting. I have to go to My Second Coming and judge the living and the dead right afterwards, and I want to be able to fit into My old raiment." ∅

Cardboard Snowflake Half-Heartedly Masking-Taped To Break-Room Door

CHRISTMAS EXPOSED

Christmas Pageant Enters Pre-Production

SAGINAW, MI—With the holiday season in full swing, the St. John's Lutheran Church Annual Christmas Pageant went into pre-production Monday. "We just hired a set builder and a location scout, and I'm looking for leads on a Mary Magdalene, because Mrs. Halverson is out with the gout this year," said church deacon Paul Verriter. "Now, all we need to do is wait for Pastor Dave [Genzler] to give his final notes on the script, and we're off and running." Verriter said he needs Genzler's approval before he can hire a team of writers to punch up the arrival of the shepherds.

Marital Frustrations Channeled Through Thermostat

DULUTH, MN—Continuing a decades-long pattern of displacement, Carl and Barb Kulick channeled their marital frustrations through their home's Honeywell T87 manual-control thermostat Monday.

The medium through which their mutual resentment is channeled.

"You should have heard Carl scream when he saw I turned the heat on today," said the understimulated, affection-starved Barb, 62. "It was chilly, and our grandson Cory was over. There's no reason for a 4-year-old boy to feel like he's freezing to death, is there? I didn't think so, but apparently, somebody around here thinks there is."

To anyone familiar with Carl's long-standing rule that the Kulick thermostat stay securely in the "off" position until November, Barb's use of it could be interpreted as an act of defiance.

"There's no need to turn it on yet," said Carl, 64, who for 20 years has strongly suspected that his wife had an affair with neighbor Phil Tewksbury in 1981. "It's a goddamn waste of money. That woman acts like we're made of money."

> "'There's no reason for a 4-year-old boy to feel like he's freezing to death, is there? I didn't think so, but apparently, somebody around here thinks there is.'"

On numerous occasions, Barb has pointed out the illogic of tying thermostat use to a date rather than temperature. Carl, however, stands firmly by his Nov. 1 start date. As the family's sole breadwinner, working long hours at a cement-supply company, Carl said it is his right to make the rules and his duty to protect the family from Barb's "dingbat notions."

"If I didn't put my foot down, Barb would have that thing turned up to 100 all the time," Carl said. "She'd have the heat on in the middle of summer and a fan blowing it out the window."

Barb's having "no concept of the value of the dollar" is just one of Carl's many dissatisfactions with his wife. He also feels she is not as bright as him, has annoying friends, and lacks personal ambition. He has also always resented her failure to bear him a son, having given birth to four girls.

Barb has complaints about Carl, as well, including his emotional inaccessibility, his refusal to include her in major household decisions, and his inability to "let loose and have fun."

"I am married to a big bump on a log," Barb said. "Other women go out dancing and get flowers. I don't even get a present on our anniversary unless I buy something for the both of us."

The thermostat is ground zero for a battle of wills all winter, with Barb silently turning the thermostat up and Carl yelling loudly as he turns it down and commands her not to "futz with it."

"I tell Barb to turn the thermostat down to 63 before she leaves the house, and she can't even remember that one thing," Carl said. "She says she forgets. That's a load of bull puckey, she forgets."

According to the couple's now-grown children, it was always easy to tell when their parents weren't getting along.

"As kids, we could tell something was up whenever ice started forming on the windows," said Deborah Wickson, 37, the couple's eldest daughter. "Mom was always edging the thermostat up half a degree at a time. Then, Dad would come in and do the same thing in reverse. He'd even get up in the middle of the night just to double-check that he'd turned it down before going to bed."

It seems unlikely that the thermostat war will end anytime soon. In fact, the situation seems to be getting worse.

"Do you know how much the price of water has gone up in the last few years?" Carl asked. "You should see the bill. How we use so much hot water in this house, I'll never know."

With the kids gone and the house paid for, Barb said that she and Carl can afford life's little luxuries.

> ## "'If I didn't put my foot down, Barb would have that thing turned up to 100 all the time,' Carl said. 'She'd have the heat on in the middle of summer and a fan blowing it out the window.'"

"I worked hard all my life, too, raising the kids. Not that Carl would notice," Barb said. "Now, I think it's time to enjoy ourselves a little bit—buy some new curtains, turn the heat up, even leave the Christmas lights on overnight instead of turning them out after the news."

While she said she would never intentionally waste energy, Barb admitted she is "forgetful sometimes" when it comes to conserving resources.

"Last winter, I baked some pies and put them out to cool on top of the deep freeze," Barb said. "Well, I must have left the oven on with nothing in it, because when Carl got home from work and found it, he came barreling down to the basement where I was doing laundry."

"His face was as red as a tomato and, boy, was he cursing up a storm," added Barb, holding back a smile. ✐

Winterizing Tips

Winter, the season of sledding and snowmen, can be lots of fun—if you prepare in advance. Here are some tips on getting ready for the cold:

- If your heat is turned off, remember: In a pinch you can cut open your fat spouse and sleep in his/her 98.6° abdominal cavity.

- Use phrases like "I love you" and "You are special to me" to create warm feelings in home.

- Check anti-freeze level if ice build-up becomes a problem in beverages.

- Be sure to caulk all drafty orifices.

- This winter, heat things up with "Red-Hot Friday Late-Nites" on Cinemax.

- Encase your car battery in a warm glow of positive reinforcement by visualizing it bathed in a nurturing, healing light.

- If absolutely necessary, it is considered acceptable to slay and eat your dogsled team.

- Heat comes from fire; make sure your house is made of materials that burn.

- Cover your home stereo system with weather-resistant tape—this will prevent Old Man Edgar Winter from gaining a foothold.

- Grow thick layer of fur on body.

- Cover tongue with special Gore-Tex sock before tasting icy metal poles.

- Enjoy a hot beverage from time to time.

- If flying above the Andes Mountains this winter season, bring along plenty of extra Paraguayan soccer players "just in case."

- Plug up crevices of house with mixture of sheep dung and straw.

- Save fatty parts of whales and seals to use as fuel.

- Master the art of hibernation by developing an enzyme that breaks down urea and other potentially poisonous chemicals created by the body during dormancy.

Top Temporary Holiday Stores

Don't-Tell-The-Cops
Independence Day M-80 Emporium

Martin Luther Mattress King

The Post-Christmas Christmas Store
(formerly The Christmas Store)

Everything's Religious And A Dollar

Sweet Christ!™
America's #1 Easter Candy Outlet

Rising Home-Heating Costs Hitting Reptile Families Hardest

CHICAGO—With government figures indicating double-digit home-heating cost increases in coming months, America's reptilian citizens are warning that, unless swift measures are taken to provide them with adequate warmth, many will face serious metabolic crises this winter.

"Unlike our mammalian citizens, who maintain a consistent body temperature and have the option of throwing on a sweater, reptiles are entirely dependent on external heat sources," Sen. Richard Durbin (D-IL) said. "All my constituents are facing rate hikes of 21 percent or more. But some of them, like it or not, may be forced into a quasi-hibernative state if they do not receive emergency fuel-price relief."

According to Department of Energy data, households in northern states have seen their home-heating bills double or even triple in recent winters. Heating costs in reptilian households have quadrupled the cost of special U.V. light bulbs.

Reaction in the reptile community has been uncharacteristically jittery.

"I don't ask for the average American to understand my lifestyle," said Arthur Marsters, 141, a cost-benefit analyst for Prudential Financial in Boston. "But there's no changing the fact that I am a giant tortoise. If I cannot maintain my core temperature, I cannot be a productive member of society, nor can I provide for my wife and latest clutch of hatchlings."

> **"'People think we're lazy, spending all summer sunning ourselves on rocks and our winters in cozy burrows,' said Mary Lou Keller, a cosmetologist and coral snake."**

Marsters was not alone in his concern for the well-being of his loved ones. Anxieties are running deep in a community that, while close-knit, cannot huddle together for warmth.

"People think we're lazy, spending all summer sunning ourselves on rocks and our winters in cozy burrows," said Mary Lou Keller, a cosmetologist and coral snake who moved to New England from Florida as a packing-crate stowaway three years ago. "But no one ever sees a reptile on food stamps. And you never see a fat one, unless it has just swallowed something whole."

Although home-heating assistance programs for needy families are available throughout the country, some reptile advocates such as Sen. Jack Reed (D-RI) argue that the application process is unfairly geared toward humans.

"Reptiles regularly apply for the needed benefits, but their tendency to react slowly means that their paperwork often misses the prescribed deadlines," Reed said. "Last year, we all heard the distressing reports of entire skink families relocating under stoves."

Reed—who owes his congressional seat to the crocodile vote and has extensive support from the terrarium, gravel, and pellet industries—is calling for heating-cost subsidies and tax credits for any vertebrate quadruped citizen who lays eggs.

"Natural-gas costs have doubled; heating-oil prices had their biggest spike in five years," Reed said. "I had an iguana in my office the other day who told me he had to take on a second job as a hippie's pet to ensure that his young have enough heat and lettuce this winter. This poor creature has enough problems maintaining a proper body temperature; now he's forced to be an absentee dad to his kids? That's just not right." Ø

Members of the Whitlow family of Elgin, IL, who have struggled to maintain their body temperatures this winter.

Parent Mad 6-Year-Old Didn't Like *Peanuts* Special

ROSE HILL, VA—Bruce Pillard, 34, was angered Tuesday over his 6-year-old daughter's indifferent reaction to *A Charlie Brown Christmas*. "That show is a classic and an annual tradition!" an incensed Pillard told daughter Courtney after watching the program on CBS. "It is not 'boring,' and the voices do not sound 'weird.' What the hell is wrong with you?" Courtney was sent to her room for the remainder of the evening.

Most Popular Winter Holiday Decorations

Hetero mistletoe — 11%

Bitterly strung popcorn — 5%

Some sort of ancient Israelite action-figure farm play set — 13%

Menorah dad welded in prison — 2%

Life-size reindeer that it is never to be sat upon — 24%

Happy Meal tie-in plush ornaments of mice Gus and Jaq from 1987 *Cinderella* rerelease — 45%

Preparing for Winter

As the mercury drops, what are Americans doing to prepare for the coming cold?

16%
Seal all orifices with caulk

23%
Stapling pink polyurethane foam to exposed areas of face and neck

31%
Filling the pantry with walnuts and acorns

37%
Slathering their bodies with insulating walrus fat/human urine mixture

42%
Substituting "Hey, ain't it hot outside" with "Hey, ain't it cold outside" in casual conversation

Winter Tip: For added traction, attach chains to feet.

Ho, Ho, Ho! I Saw You Masturbating!

Season's greetings from your old friend Santa! My, oh, my, only 12 nights left until Christmas Eve! Things are getting so close now, we can hardly contain ourselves here at the North Pole. And from the looks of it, my young friend, we're not the only ones set to burst! Why, Jolly Old Saint Nick hasn't seen a Yule log this lit in ages!

Now, don't be shy. You know what Santa's talking about. You just couldn't wait to open your present this year, could you? Ho, ho, ho! Dear child, I saw you masturbating!

And it hasn't been just once either! Oh, no! Santa's seen you at least twice splashing away in the bathtub, three times in the attic with one of your mother's old art-history books, and more times than even he can count spread out like a stunned partridge on that beanbag chair of yours!

Why, old Santa might just have a heart attack if he popped out your chimney on that cold winter's night and, instead of milk and cookies, found his dear little pen pal shamefully hunched over the family computer.

Oh, what a naughty, prolific rascal you've been!

You see, dear lad, Santa's been keeping a list. Just like the one you keep in your head of all your favorite classmates. The one you've checked so much more than twice. Except when Santa thinks about his list, he doesn't rub his crotch feverishly against the smooth contours of his writing desk. Ho, ho, ho!

> **"Yes, I suppose you could say old Kris Kringle knows everything there is to know. Well, not *everything*. You did teach me a thing or two about scented body wash! Ho, Ho, ho!"**

I see you when you're sleeping, child, and I know when you're awake. And, believe it or not, I even know when you're just pretending to sleep, but really have your rosy palms down the front of your britches.

Yes, I suppose you could say old Kris Kringle knows everything there is to know. Well, not *everything*. You did teach me a thing or two about scented body wash! Ho, ho, ho!

Tell me now, what do you want Santa to bring you this year? A bright red bicycle? Some fun new board games? Or should I just have the elves wrap up a fresh batch of those satin pillows you enjoy straddling so much? Or maybe St. Nick shouldn't bring you anything at all this Christmas. After all, Mrs. Claus knitted you a special pair of socks last year, and just look what became of those!

Oh, whatever happened to that sweet, freckle-faced angel we all loved so much?

Such a bright little youngster, so good to your mommy and daddy, and quick to make friends. Now all you seem to want to do is play by yourself for hours on end. It makes everyone here at my workshop very, very sad. Why, the reindeer haven't been able to keep down their feed since hearing about how you slap yourself around. And Mrs. Claus, do you know what she did when she found out? She cried. She cried for the first time in almost 700 years.

"Tell me now, what do you want Santa to bring you this year? A bright red bicycle? Some fun new board games? Or should I just have the elves wrap up a fresh batch of those satin pillows you enjoy straddling so much?"

Where before we enjoyed visions of gumdrops and candy canes, now we see you, once so dear to us all, kneeling against a plastic chair, spitting on two fingers, and putting them lordy knows where.

I must say, the sights you conjure up while you lie in your bed have even Santa Claus scratching his head. I doubt any of the high-school cheerleaders have ever even set foot inside a boiler room before, never mind done anything like that!

And other things—other terrible, frightful things. If your outlandish fantasies didn't make me quake with disgust, I'd say you were the most creative child in the world.

Is it Clara? Is that who you think about when you rub yourself raw? Ho, ho, ho! Why she doesn't even know your name, dear child! You didn't really think you had a chance with her, did you? A pretty girl like that? But your face—it's covered in pockmarks, for goodness sake!

Don't cry now, little one. I'm sure some of the Barbie dolls you steal from your sister's room find you very attractive. I bet they hardly even notice your embarrassing stutter, or that pungent and sickly body odor of yours. Or even how pathetic you really are, my child. What a sad, lonely, feeble little shit you are, and how your life—your wretched little life—will be filled with failure after failure, both personal and professional, until the stench of disappointment and heartbreak grows so strong that you'll barely be able to breathe.

Well, it looks like old Santa has to get back to work! Happy Christmas to all, and to all a good night—except you, you sick little fuck! *Ø*

DECEMBER 24, 2009 · VOLUME 45 ISSUE 52

AMERICA'S FINEST NEWS SOURCE · ONION.COM · NATIONAL EDITION

the ONION

Celebrates The Holidays

INSIDE

We Were Going To Run A Photo With Seth Rogen, Paul Rudd, And Jonah Hill As The Three Wise Men, But The Money Fell Through

THE JOY OF GIVING
How Much Is Too Much?

PLUS

The Weird Mormon Version Of The Holidays You Didn't Know About

A.V. CLUB

Our annual round-up of the year's least essential albums

WE VAGUELY OBSCURE OUR CLEAR CHRISTIAN BIAS BY SAYING

دیع دیع عس

$2.00 US | $3.00 CAN

INSIDE: Essayist Ronald Hughes On The Smell Of Christmas—That Sickening Pine Smell—And All The Misery It Evokes

Ø the ONION® STATSHOT

Hot Holiday Toys

1. Ball-Point Pen! The Game Where You Can Write Stuff
2. Hemorrhaging Hemorrhaging Hippos
3. Gail - Barbie's Friend With The Good Personality
4. Arbeit Macht Fun! The Ant Farm Where You Work 'Em To Death
5. Baby Shitsitself

Broke Dad Makes Son PlayStation 2 For Christmas

DAYTON, OH—Determined to make his son's Christmas dreams come true despite financial woes, David McManus spent three hours in his garage Monday constructing a PlayStation 2 from scrap lumber and transistor-radio components. "I can't wait to see the look on Andy's face when he unwraps this," said McManus, lovingly painting a "2" onto the front of the handmade video-game console. "I didn't get to sand the controllers as smoothly as I'd have liked, but still." McManus added that he hopes he can make a "Tony Hawk's Pro Skater 2" CD in time for Andy's birthday in March.

Activist Judge Cancels Christmas

WASHINGTON, DC—In a sudden and unexpected blow to the Americans working to protect the holiday, liberal U.S. 9th Circuit Court of Appeals Judge Stephen Reinhardt ruled the private celebration of Christmas unconstitutional Monday.

"In accordance with my activist agenda to secularize the nation, this court finds Christmas to be unlawful," Judge Reinhardt said. "The celebration of the birth of the philosopher Jesus—be it in the form of gift-giving, the singing of carols, fanciful decorations, or general good cheer and warm feelings amongst families—is in violation of the First Amendment principles upon which this great nation was founded."

In addition to forbidding the celebration of Christmas in any form, Judge Reinhardt has made it illegal to say "Merry Christmas." Instead, he has ruled that Americans must say "Happy Holidays" or "Felices Fiestas" if they wish to extend good tidings.

Within an hour of the judge's verdict, National Guard troops were mobilized to enforce the controversial ruling.

"Sorry, kids, no Christmas this year," Beloit, WI, mall Santa Gene Ernot said as he was led away from his Santa's Village in leg irons. "Write to your congressman to put a stop to these liberal activist judges. It's up to you to save Christmas! Ho ho ho!"

Said Pvt. Stanley Cope, who tasered Ernot for his outburst: "We're fighting an unpopular war on Christmas, but what can we do? The military has no choice but to take orders from a lone activist judge."

Across America, the decision of the all-powerful liberal courts was met with shock and disappointment, as American families

Per the court order, city workers take down the Christmas tree from New York's Rockefeller Plaza.

CHRISTMAS EXPOSED

quietly took down their holiday decorations and canceled their plans to gather and make merry.

> ## "Shortly after Dover issued his statement, police kicked down his door, removed his holiday tree, confiscated his presents, and crushed his homemade card underfoot."

"They've been chipping away at Christmas rights for decades," Fox News personality John Gibson said. "Even before this ruling, you couldn't hear a Christmas song on the radio or in a department store. I hate to say it, America, but I told you so."

Gibson then went into hiding, vowing to be a vital part of the Christmas resistance that would eventually triumph and bring Christmas back to the United States and its retail stores.

The ban is not limited to the retail sector. In support of Reinhardt's ruling, Sen. Ted Kennedy, a Jew, introduced legislation that would mandate the registration of every Christian in the United States and subject their houses to random searches to ensure they are not celebrating Christmas.

"Getting rid of every wreath or nativity scene is not enough," Kennedy said. "In order to ensure that Americans of every belief feel comfortable in any home or business, we must eliminate all traces of this offensive holiday. My yellow belly quakes with fear at the thought of offending any foreigners, atheists, or child molesters."

America's children are bearing the brunt of Reinhardt's marginal, activist rulings.

"Why did the bad man take away Christmas?" 5-year-old Danny Dover said. "I made a card for my mommy out of paper and glue, and now I can't give it to her."

Shortly after Dover issued his statement, police kicked down his door, removed his holiday tree, confiscated his presents, and crushed his homemade card underfoot.

> ## "'They've been chipping away at Christmas rights for decades. Even before this ruling, you couldn't hear a Christmas song on the radio or in a department store. I hate to say it, America, but I told you so.'"

A broad, bipartisan coalition of lawmakers has been working closely with the White House, banding together in the hope of somehow overruling the decision. So far, however, their efforts have been fruitless.

"Our hearts go out to the Americans this ruling affects," Sen. Chip Pickering (R-MS) said. "If it's any condolence, I wish you all a Happy Holidays, which, I'm afraid, is all I'm legally allowed to say at this time." *Ⓖ*

Cretinous Reprobate Home For The Holidays

MONTPELIER, VT—Mark Wilens, a 41-year-old cretinous reprobate who relocated to California six years ago, is back home in Vermont for the holidays, it was reported Monday. "The pudding is on the table, the fire is roaring, and Mark is here with his family," said Lila Wilens, mother of the unctuous, deceitful shit. "Hopefully, we'll get a chance to go caroling while he's home, on one of the days when he's not hanging out by the Catholic school with his binoculars." The filthy pig last spent Christmas with his loved ones in 1995.

The Online Shopping Boom

Online consumer sales are expected to total $6.1 billion in 1998, rising to $20 billion by 2000. Why are so many Americans kissing their malls goodbye?

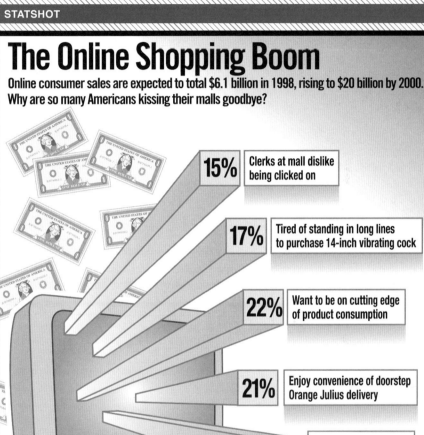

15% Clerks at mall dislike being clicked on

17% Tired of standing in long lines to purchase 14-inch vibrating cock

22% Want to be on cutting edge of product consumption

21% Enjoy convenience of doorstep Orange Julius delivery

25% Similar to watching TV, with added attraction of spending money

95 Percent Of Opinions Withheld On Visit To Family

KALAMAZOO, MI–A full 95 percent of the opinions held by Justin Wilmot, 26, were kept to himself Sunday during a visit with his family.

Wilmot holds his tongue while his sister and mother discuss their mutual excitement about *Legally Blonde 2.*

"No one in my family really gets my worldview, so I find it easier just to smile and nod and agree with everything," Wilmot said Monday. "When I'm with them, I tend to be a lot quieter than when I'm hanging out with friends."

Wilmot, who grew up in Kalamazoo and now lives in Chicago, described the visit as "seven hours of self-censorship."

"We're totally not on the same wavelength at all," Wilmot said. "I'm not just talking about dangerous subjects like politics or religion, but pretty much everything they bring up–the shows they watch, the things they buy, the people they know. So if someone says *Daddy Day Care* was hilarious, I may be thinking, 'I can't believe Eddie Murphy was once respected as a subversive comic genius,' but I sure as hell don't say it."

Among the subjects Wilmot declined to weigh in on during the weekend get-together: new Tropical Sprite, *Survivor*, the selfishness of childless couples, Iraq, golf, AM talk radio, and his brother-in-law's fan-

tastic idea for a calling-card side business.

Wilmot said he used to voice his opinions, but has long since given up.

"There was a time when my sister would mention how much she wants an SUV, and I'd be unable to resist launching into a whole thing about how irresponsible and wasteful they are. But after receiving my thousandth blank, confused stare from everybody at the table, I realized it was futile," Wilmot said. "Now, I don't even flinch when my dad mentions he's reading 'this amazing book called *The Celestine Prophecy*.' That's how bad it is."

> **"'My brother-in-law belongs to the NRA, which used to appall me. Well, it still appalls me, but now I'm appalled silently.'"**

In the course of Sunday's meal, Wilmot estimated that he heard 100 statements he could have strenuously contested. Instead, he responded with such neutral phrases as, "Cool," "Uh-huh," "Wow," "I know," "Definitely," and "Oh, good."

"My brother-in-law belongs to the NRA, which used to appall me," Wilmot said. "Well, it still appalls me, but now I'm appalled silently. Same goes for my mom's assertion that El Taco Loco is 'the best Mexican restaurant in town.' I don't even bother mentioning Arturo's, this little place over on Third Street that's the only authentic Mexican place in all of Kalamazoo. I'm sure she's never heard of it."

When he was young, Wilmot actually

enjoyed engaging his family in debate, but now he would rather smile pleasantly as his brother's wife talks about the latest exciting arrival on the local shopping scene.

"Meredith said they're putting up a huge new Target Greatland right by their house," Wilmot said. "She says she's psyched because Target is way better than Wal-Mart. I just nodded and said, 'Yeah, totally.'"

"Once you let go of the need to express your thoughts to your family, you suddenly feel much lighter," Wilmot said. "You just float along blissfully, finally liberated from the burden of having any presence at all. It's sort of like getting to return to the womb. Which is way more enjoyable than trying to explain to a tableful of Celine Dion fans why you can't stand her." ∅

Coal Now Too Expensive To Put In Christmas Stockings

CHICAGO—With winter's onset driving the demand for surface coal to record-high levels, the mineral's cost is now beyond the reach of low- and middle-income Americans who wish to punish their naughty children. "Coal in one's stocking is meant to serve as an admonishment or warning, not as a dependable grade-B investment," said William Menchell, a commodities adviser for T. Rowe Price. "In today's market, children should have their stockings stuffed with lumps of coal only if they have been studious and obedient, and they show an interest in long-term investments in the energy sector." For more affordable punitive options, analysts point to the relatively stagnant switch market, which could soon go the way of coal if demand increases for combustible wooden sticks.

Santa Claus Killed In Electric-Razor Crash

STAMFORD, CT—Noted philanthropic elf Santa Claus was killed Monday in an electric-razor crash during a practice run for his annual global gift delivery. According to witnesses, at 11:20 p.m., while riding over an icy embankment, Claus lost control of the Norelco razor he was piloting, sending him careening into a suburban home. Long believed immortal, Claus was pulled from the mangled razor and rushed to a local hospital, where he was pronounced dead. "We are shocked and saddened by this tragedy," Norelco CEO Steve Drucker said. "This is a terrible loss, not only for the Norelco family, but for all the children of the world." Control of KringCo, Santa's massive non-profit toy-distribution franchise, was transferred to former Secretary of State Henry Kissinger, widely known to possess the same magic powers as Claus. Children are advised that Dr. Kissinger prefers "a nice green salad or fruit plate" to cookies.

Another Lousy Christ-mas

How appropriate, during the season in which we celebrate the glorious nativity of our Holy Savior the Christ-Child, that I

By T. Herman Zweibel, Publisher Emeritus (Photo circa 1911)

found my-self the proud papa of my own sweet little son! Giddy over the blessed arrival of N. Aeschylus, I vowed that the Zweibel clan's annual Christ-mas pageant and talent exhibition would be especially lavish. I instructed my man-servant Standish to assemble the finest entertainment in the Republic and to set up the old Nativity scene props. It would truly be a Yule to remember!

Unfortunately, the affair proved a disaster from the start. Shortly before the jubilee was to begin, I received a cable from my sweet-heart and mother of my child, Miss Bernadette Fiske, saying that she and the baby would not be able to attend the festivities, as her town was thoroughly snowed in and no trains were able to depart. It was a keen disappointment, as I was hoping to see both little N. Aeschylus and Miss Fiske for the very first time, and I wanted the little shaver to play Baby Jesus in our traditional Nativity pantomime tableau. But instead of canceling every-thing, I simply filled in for my son, and as I took my place inside the straw-filled manger, I declared the festivities open. "Bring on the entertainment!" I commanded.

The first act was none other than my own eunuch, Sandy, who performed the beloved and poignant carol "O Holy Night." But rather than moving us to tears, Sandy's disturbingly girlish soprano only managed to pierce every-one's ear-drums. I knew I should have mailed that eunuch back to Araby or where-ever he's from ages ago!

The second performer was a lady who billed her-self as a "performance artist." As she recited a lengthy diatribe about the "unfair patriarchy" and "systematic oppression of women," she stripped naked and proceeded to smear her-self with candied yams. I was out-raged. She completely stole her act from Fanny Brice! I remember seeing this exact routine in the Ziegfeld Follies of 1917. I stopped the act short and had her hauled off the stage through the use of a elongated cane.

> **"'Sandy's disturbingly girlish soprano only managed to pierce every-one's ear-drums. I knew I should have mailed that eunuch back to Araby or where-ever he's from ages ago!'"**

The third performer was a comic monologuist, but the moment he began talking some gibberish about the poor quality of "air-line food," I promptly ended the festivities. Another Christ-mas ruined, and I blame this, as I blame all misfortune in my life, on the American people. Screw you all to the last man! I hope you all choke on your figgy pudding! ✑

MIT Think-Tank Develops 20 Great Gift Ideas

CAMBRIDGE, MA—Twelve math and science professors at a Massachusetts Institute of Technology think-tank announced their latest brainstorming success Monday: 20 great holiday gift ideas for the co-worker or loved one who seems to have everything. "We dedicated ourselves to solving this most universal of problems," said team leader and biochemistry professor Charles J. Chang, "and we are proud to say we have come up with 20 great solutions." Among the ideas: a T-shirt reading, "It's Not a Beer Gut, It's a Gas Tank For a Sex Machine," available at Spencer Gifts; a hand-held electronic golf game from The Sharper Image; and a Corvette-shaped videotape rewinder from the Suncoast Motion Picture Company. "You can rewind your tapes in it," said team member Dr. Phillip Wasserstein. "Most people rewind them in their VCRs, but if you have one of these, you won't have to."

Man Braves Freezing Weather To Cross Parking Lot

LANCASTER, PA—Surmounting treacherous icy pavement and a windchill factor dipping as low as 19 degrees Fahrenheit, local resident Louis Bergstrom survived a real-life battle with the elements Friday when he successfully completed a harrowing four-and-a-half-minute journey across the desolate, frozen parking lot of an area G & G Grocery Store, the 38-year-old court stenographer told reporters.

According to Bergstrom, with night coming and temperatures dropping rapidly, he was forced to leave his wife, Linda, 37, at the entrance of the supermarket and valiantly set out on his own to retrieve the couple's 2001 Toyota Corolla. Before leaving, Bergstrom solemnly vowed that he would return for his pregnant wife as soon as he possibly could.

Recuperating at home following his struggle with nature's fury, a visibly shaken Bergstrom recounted the look in his wife's eyes at the moment he set out across the barren rows of the parking lot.

"I could see that she was concerned, but I wasn't about to let Linda go out there," a blanket-wrapped Bergstrom said from the safety of his living room couch between sips of hot chocolate. "She'd left her hat at home."

Shivering from the brutal winds, his heart full of determination, Bergstrom encountered the first setback on his grueling 75-meter trek when a sudden gust of

The cold and unforgiving backdrop of Bergstrom's four-and-a-half-minute bout with death.

wind blew freezing cold snow off an SUV and down his collar, nearly causing him to lose his footing on the slippery pavement. Due to the restrictive nature of his bulky cold-weather gear, several tense seconds passed before Bergstrom was able to brush the snow out of his jacket and soldier on.

Bergstrom's next hardship came when he was forced to guide the wheels of his shopping cart through the increasingly slushy terrain. He was eventually left with no choice but to abandon the cart and carry nearly seven pounds of his own groceries in hand for the remainder of the journey, slogging past the lifeless, long-abandoned carts of those who had attempted the perilous journey before him.

"I remember thinking, 'If I stay out here much longer, I'm going to freeze to death,'" Bergstrom said. "It was that cold."

Because the strain of his journey at times caused him to doubt whether he would ever find his car, Bergstrom said he was forced to look inward—drawing strength from past experiences in which he successfully overcame similar extreme conditions. No stranger to long waits on hold for customer service or scaling the heights of the attic stairs with nothing but a box of Christmas decorations, Bergstrom recounted one traumatic ordeal in which he was locked out of his own home during a violent rainstorm for a full 12 minutes before his wife heard him knocking.

However, even with all of his experience, nothing could have prepared Bergstrom for what was in store for him next.

"I thought I saw my car, but it was a different Corolla about seven spaces up," remembered Bergstrom, who, upon seeing the similar Toyota, made the near-tragic mistake of removing one of his gloves in order to retrieve his keys and accidentally dropping it beneath the misidentified vehicle.

With visibility limited by blowing snow and the fast-approaching dusk, Bergstrom was forced to leave the glove behind. Summoning all his strength, he quickly reoriented himself, using the brightly lit Blockbuster Video store to the right of the supermarket as a guide, and steadily made his way in the general direction of his car.

After one-and-a-half tense minutes, the Pennsylvania native made the ingenious tactical decision to set down his shopping bags and blow vigorously into his unprotected fingers, providing him with just enough warmth to retrieve his bags and continue on.

"He was eventually left with no choice but to abandon the cart and carry nearly seven pounds of his own groceries in hand for the remainder of the journey."

"Those final twenty feet were the hardest," Bergstrom said of the journey. "That last thirty seconds felt like an eternity out there."

Chilled to the core, Bergstrom at last reached safety and collapsed exhausted behind the wheel. His survival instincts kicking in, he swiftly put his key into the ignition, turned the heat up "full blast," hit the defrost button, and waited for the car to warm up. He then set about recouping his energies before undertaking the only remaining task: retrieving his ice scraper from the glove compartment and leaving the car one final time to begin the painstaking and risky process of removing the thick layer of ice from the car windows.

Shaken but wiser after the ordeal, Bergstrom said that he is "just glad to be home again," but that, if nothing else, he has learned a valuable life lesson he will not likely forget.

"I don't think I've ever been so cold in my life," Bergstrom said. "I'm parking much closer next time—even if I have to circle that parking lot several times to find a space." Ø

Vatican Employees Unable To Relax At Holiday Party With Pope Around

VATICAN CITY—According to various cardinals and nuns attending the Vatican's holiday party last night, festivities were made awkward by the unexpected appearance of Pope Benedict XVI. "[Prefect Emeritus] Bernardin [Gantin] was about to bust out his St. Bridget impression, which is just spot on, but then the pope walked over and we quickly changed the subject to the sacred presence of the Holy Spirit during transubstantiation," said a cardinal speaking on the condition of anonymity, adding that Pope Benedict's "way too formal" attire made everyone feel even more ill at ease. "He said he didn't want to talk about work, but guess who was the first one to make a segue from our favorite local restaurants to the Bangorian Controversy with the Church Of England?" Several Vatican employees recalled "the good old days" when Pope John Paul II turned a blind eye to their attempts to get the secretaries drunk playing "Never Have I Ever."

Furby Fever

The "Furby," a high-tech, interactive stuffed toy, is all the rage this Christmas season. What is its appeal?

20%
Fills longtime consumer need for animal that is both furry and beaked

25%
Furby's high-powered processors, servomotors and infrared sensors can be combined with kids' bathwater for lucrative insurance claims

19%
Learns English interactively over time, unlike real kids

15%
Scored much higher with focus groups than rival "wire-mother" toy

14%
Provides long-desired lust outlet for nation's 22 million furbisexuals

7%
Can be trained to kill silently

Congress' Pre-Christmas Cuts

The House recently voted to cut $1.6 billion in social-program spending right before Christmas. What do *you* think?

Babette Layton
Police Officer

"Well, isn't this
in keeping with
the true spirit of
Congress?"

Nick Cardy
Web Press Operator

"Christmas is a
time for fellow-
ship and good will
towards men, not
a lot of negativity
about who is or
isn't able to afford
food or heat."

Mike Royer
Furniture Restoration
Expert

"Geez, you people
are never happy.
If the House voted
to cut $1.6 billion
in social programs
in the late spring,
you would say
they were ruining
people's summer."

Out-Of-Control Revelers Deck Shit Out Of Area Halls

AMES, IA—Holiday celebrations took an extreme turn Saturday as an unruly mob of out-of-control holiday revelers observed the shit out of the Christmas season, violently decking 11 area halls.

According to police reports, at approximately 9 p.m., after consuming large quantities of 60-proof eggnog, the frenzied throng of 40 to 50 revelers broke into the home of Ames resident Milton Krajcek, aggressively decking his halls with wreaths, garlands, ribbons, ceramic nativity scenes, tree ornaments, mistletoe, candy canes, and "shitloads" of boughs of holly.

Once their supplies were exhausted, the crazed merrymakers rode in pickup trucks to a local ShopKo outlet to restock, only to return and continue decking the already overburdened halls.

> **"'Look at my halls. I can barely squeeze through there, such was the force and vigor of their decking.'"**

The aftermath of Saturday's brutal hall-decking spree. The revelers responsible are still at large.

"I begged them to stop," Krajcek said, "but they wouldn't until every last inch of my halls was decked beyond all recognition."

> **"The wanted celebrants are described as inebriated suburbanites clad in gay apparel, which they allegedly 'donned the holy living fuck out of,' according to Pfeiffer. Added the police chief: 'We have reason to believe they may be armed and extremely joyous.'"**

Not satisfied with forcibly festooning Krajcek's halls, the slavering, cheerful horde then turned to those of other locals, posing as holiday carolers to lure residents to their doors.

"I heard an ancient yuletide carol coming from the front porch," said Millicent Slopes, 53, "and was pretty worried because they were really tolling the hell out of it. I decided to acknowledge them so that maybe they would leave, but as soon as I opened the door, they poured into my house and went batshlt on the halls. Look at my halls. I can barely squeeze through there, such was the force and vigor of their decking."

"It was horrible," said Francine Eppard, whose halls were also brutally decorated. "There was tinsel everywhere."

Ames police officials are still searching for the binge revelers. If caught, they will be charged with breaking and entering, reckless and wanton decoration, second-degree festivity, and willful construction of toyland towns around six Christmas trees.

"The scum who did this will pay," police chief Carl Pfeiffer said. "No punishment could be too severe for perpetrators of this kind of senseless, senseless decking."

The wanted celebrants are described as inebriated suburbanites clad in gay apparel, which they allegedly "donned the holy living fuck out of," according to Pfeiffer. Added the police chief: "We have reason to believe they may be armed and extremely joyous."

Until the revelers are captured, Pfeiffer warned homeowners not to open their doors for carolers, strongly advising that nuts and cocoa instead be lowered from an upstairs window or pushed through a mail slot. *∅*

ONION WEEKENDER

DECEMBER 7, 2008

Holiday Gift Guide

50 Things For Your Sister That Look Like They Might Cost $75

$75 gift card

Smithsonian
David Hockney Makes a Splash

But Are Actually Promotional Items For Opening Credit Cards

INSIDE Chronic Fatigue Syndrome: Could Screaming 'Wake The Fuck Up' Help?

Fun Toy Banned Because Of Three Stupid Dead Kids

WASHINGTON, DC—In cooperation with the U.S. Consumer Product Safety Commission, Wizco Toys of Montclair, NJ, recalled 245,000 Aqua Assault RoboFighters Monday after three dumb kids managed to kill themselves playing with the popular toy, ruining the fun for everybody else.

The Aqua Assault RoboFighter, an awesome toy children can no longer enjoy.

"The tragedy is inconceivable," Wizco president Alvin Cassidy said. "For years, countless children played with the Aqua Assault RoboFighter without incident. But then these three retards come along and somehow find a way to get themselves killed. So now we have to do a full recall and halt production on what was a really awesome toy. What a waste."

"My mom won't let me play with my RoboFighter because of those dumb kids who died," said 10-year-old Jeremy Daigle of Somerville, MA. "I used to set up army guys around the RoboFighter and have it run over them and conquer Earth for the Zardaxians. But now I'll never see it again, all because three stupid idiots had to go and wreck everything."

Each of the deaths was determined to be the result of gross misuse of the toy, an incredibly cool device that could shoot both plastic missiles and long jets of water, as well as maneuver over the ground on retractable wheels.

The first death occurred June 22, when 7-year-old Isaac Weiller of Grand Junction, CO, died after deliberately firing one of the spring-loaded plastic missiles into his left nostril. The missile shot into his sinuses, shattering the roof of his nasal cavity and causing a massive brain hemorrhage.

Shortly before dying, Weiller told emergency medical personnel at St. Luke's Medical Center that he had shot the missile into his nose in the belief that it would travel through his body and out his belly button.

> "'If you're 11 years old, you should know that it's impossible to fly. And poor Wizco's probably going to go bankrupt because of this shit.'"

"I've heard some pretty stupid shit in my time, but that has to take the cake," said Dr. Anderson Hunt, the attending physician. "Why would any kid think he could fire plastic missiles up his nose and expect them to come out his belly button? There's no point in feeling bad about this child's demise, because the deck was obviously stacked against him from the start. What

Joshua Schatzeder of Grand Rapids, MI, is forced to play with a boring little fire truck as a result of the recall.

we should feel bad about is the fact that because of him, millions of other children will no longer get to fire the RoboFighter's super-cool Devastator Missiles or soak their friends with its FunFoam WaterBlasters."

Less than one month after Weiller's death, 5-year-old Danielle Krug fatally suffocated on fragments of the toy after repeatedly smashing it with a claw hammer in the garage of her parents' La Porte, IN, home.

"I'm not kidding," said Dianne Ensor, an emergency-room nurse at Our Lady Of Peace Hospital in La Porte, where Krug was pronounced dead. "She thought the broken shards were candy. That's what you'd assume after breaking a plastic, inedible toy, right? Absolutely un-fucking-believable."

The third and arguably stupidest death occurred August 12, when 11-year-old dumbass Michael Torres held the RoboFighter above his head and jumped off the balcony of his family's third-story Torrance, CA, apartment, thinking he would be able to fly like Superman.

"A couple of my fellow emergency workers thought we should cut the kid some slack, because at least he wasn't trying to eat the toy or shove it up his nose," said paramedic Debra Lindfors, who tried in vain to revive Torres. "I considered this for a while, but then I decided no. No way. If you're 11 years old, you should know that it's impossible to fly. And poor Wizco's probably going to go bankrupt because of this shit."

"'I'm not kidding. She thought the broken shards were candy. That's what you'd assume after breaking a plastic, inedible toy, right? Absolutely un-fucking-believable.'"

As a result of the extreme idiocy of the three children, the CPSC was forced to order Wizco to stop making the toy and remove it from store shelves, as well as recommend that parents remove it from their homes.

"I know the overwhelming majority of American kids who owned an Aqua Assault RoboFighter derived many hours of safe, responsible fun from it," CPSC commissioner Mary Sheila Gall said. "But, statistically speaking, three deaths stemming from contact with a particular toy constitutes an 'unreasonable risk.' Look, I'm really sorry about this. Honestly. But our agency's job is to protect the public from hazardous products, even if those who die are morons who deserved what they got." Ø

World Inspired By First Snowman To Win Luge

VANCOUVER—In what has become the most inspiring story at the XXI Winter Olympiad, the luge was won Sunday by the most unlikely of competitors: Tom, a snowman rolled together just two days earlier by the Kansy family of Vancouver. "Another barrier falls, marking a historic day for iced people everywhere," was the call from NBC's Bob Costas as Tom took the top spot on the Olympic victory podium. "Tom has proven it matters not the composition of your skin, only whether you are capable of competing at the highest possible level. He entered these Olympics as Tom the Snowman, but history will remember him as Tom the Luger." Tom was unavailable for comment as the Kansy family had only given him a twig for a mouth.

Christmas Trees More Expensive

Due to high fuel costs, the price of Christmas trees will be around 10 percent higher this year. What do *you* think?

Terry Golden
Personal Assistant

"The high costs have affected Hanukkah, too. I could only afford a menorah with four candleholders."

Grace Patrochis
Systems Analyst

"That tricky Jesus. Always trying to make a buck."

Chuck Warner
Caddy

"I cut down my own tree every year. It makes Christmas more meaningful without the hassle of attending church."

Secret Santas Are For Shit

Hola, amigos. What's going on? I know it's been a long time since I rapped at ya, but I've been carrying a heavy load lately. The winter's really depressing the shit out of me. Between the cold and the 14 hours of darkness, I never want to leave the house. All my pals are in the same boat, so they don't come over and hang out like they usually do. Good thing I got my Game-Cube. That's all the friends I need.

The Cruise
by Jim Anchower

I did manage to find myself a gig for the month, though. There's this Christmas store called Holiday Land, where they sell all kinds of festive shit: wreaths, trees, mistletoe, and candles that are supposed to smell like cinnamon or pine but just smell like stink-candles. You probably know the place. In October, it was called Spooky World, and they sold masks and vampire fangs. I was hoping I could find all that old Halloween stuff in storage so I could snag a few tubes of fake blood, but they have this warehouse they send all the stuff back to when the season's over.

I'm in the tree department. I guess I got my wish to get a job where I can burn off some of my gut, 'cause all I do is haul crap around all day. I take people's trees and run them through this tube of nylon net so they can tie it to their car without needles and branches flying all over the place. The pay's pretty decent, and I guess everyone's all right, except my boss, Mr. Smalley. The guy's a total dickweed. He thinks he's being funny when he calls me Jim Clamchowder, like I didn't hear enough of that in eighth grade.

Last Friday, Smalley totally dressed me down for wishing someone a Merry Christmas. I told him I thought we were supposed to say that, and he was like, "You're supposed to say 'Happy Holidays.' It fosters an environment of religious inclusion." I got a news flash for you, Smalley: It don't make no difference if you tell them "Happy Ass Day." They're there to get a Christmas tree, not a holiday tree.

Then there's the whole Secret Santa thing. Smalley was all like, "Come on, it'll be fun!" Now, I've got a pretty good idea of what fun is, and some bullshit Secret Santa just doesn't make the cut. It wasn't like we were required to participate, but it was "strongly suggested." It's like peer pressure. In junior-high health class, they never had film strips about Secret Santa peer pressure, but they should've. And they should've starred Smalley, shaking a coffee can full of names in your face.

> **"That's when it hit me. Right in front, they had this huge stack of what can only be called paradise. It was a tower of 12-packs of Miller Genuine Draft that was at least as tall as me."**

I drew Nancy, this old chick at the checkout counter. I had no idea what to get her. We'd barely said three words to each other since I started working there. All I knew about her was that she smoked Newports and had an enormous rack.

The days flew by, and I kept forgetting to pick something up. The day before we were supposed to swap gifts, I thought long and hard about it on the drive home from work. It's tough work trying to figure out what to get someone you don't know and won't be working with in three weeks. It was making me thirsty, so I pulled over to the big warehouse liquor store on the way home. That's when it hit me.

Right in front, they had this huge stack of what can only be called paradise. It was a tower of 12-packs of Miller Genuine Draft that was at least as tall as me. The 12-packs were on sale for $6.50. At that price, I'd have been stupid not to get it for the Secret Santa, especially since it was definitely under the $10 spending limit. I picked one up for Nancy and grabbed three for me. I wasn't about to spread that sort of holiday cheer without getting a little for myself.

I took my treasure trove home, put one of my twelves in the fridge, and looked for some wrapping paper. All I had was a bunch of Walgreens circulars that had been piling up for, like, three months and some duct tape. After the longest 15 minutes of my life, I finally finished the wrap job. Rewarding myself for a job well done, I took out one of my beers and had a swig.

The next day, I went to the break-room table and, sure enough, there was a gift waiting for me from my Secret Santa. It was definitely too small to be beer, but maybe they got me a pint of Dr. McGillicuddy's or something. I put my package with the others and got to work.

At about 4:30, we knocked off a half-hour early so we could eat cookies and open our presents. After five or six people went, it came time for Nancy to open hers. As she started to open it, I yelled, "Hey, save the paper—I took a lot of time wrapping that!" Everyone laughed, and I knew I had it made.

As she was opening it, she had this weird look on her face. Then she started shaking. Some of the other cashiers were staring at me, giving me the stink eye. Nancy looked up at me and said thanks for the gift, but told me she'd quit drinking about four months ago. I was like, "All right! More for me!" but this time, no one

laughed. I kept to myself the rest of the "party," and every once in a while, I'd get dirty looks from the other cashiers. How was I supposed to know Nancy was on the wagon? When the party ended, I just drove home and went through the better part of one of my 12-packs.

"Shit, why not just knit me a sweater with a reindeer and the words 'Kick my ass' on it? That'd do the job just as well. Sometimes, there's no justice."

And what did I get from my Secret Santa? A red and green scarf. Man, there are so many things wrong with that. First off, Jim Anchower doesn't wear scarves. Never have, and I ain't about to break tradition just because someone got me one. Second, I never wear red and green. Shit, why not just knit me a sweater with a reindeer and the words "Kick my ass" on it? That'd do the job just as well. Sometimes, there's no justice.

But like I said, I ain't ungrateful. I'm sure my Secret Santa, Debbie from the back office, thought it was cool. We can't all be blessed with good taste. I took the scarf and threw it under my bed. At least now I have something to give if I ever get suckered into doing another Secret Santa.

New Year's Eve had better be better than Christmas is shaping up to be. That's all I'm saying. ∅

McCain Stares at Screen, Attempts To Write Family Christmas Letter

SEDONA, AZ—After procrastinating for several hours by watching *It's A Wonderful Life* and old John Wayne movies, former Republican presidential nominee John McCain finally sat down at the computer to type his annual "Christmas Bulletin" to friends and family early this afternoon, but found himself completely blocked. "They say you're never too old to learn," McCain slowly typed before pausing, reading the sentence over, and tapping the backspace key until it was deleted. Forty-five minutes later, after two aborted attempts to compose the letter from the point of view of the family cat, Oreo, and another about what 2009 held in store for the McCain clan, the Arizona senator took a break to make a cup of hot cocoa and listen to the grandfather clock ticking in the background. "Jesus," McCain mumbled. "Jesus Christ." McCain returned to the den around 5:30 p.m., at which point he placed a fresh stack of candy-cane stationery in the printer, stared at the screen for another 10 minutes, and finally decided to go to sleep for a long, long time.

Toy-Buying Tips for Parents

Not all toys are created equal. Here are some tips to help you choose playthings for your children that are safe and educational:

- Decide what you would like your child to be, then only buy toys that steer him or her in that direction.

- If it is Finnish, sold at an upscale toy boutique, and three times as expensive as a comparable toy made by an American company, it is safe and educational.

- You can never go wrong buying your child a crystal-radio set. It's a great way for him or her to learn about crystal radios.

- Often, the best toys are the simplest. For example, sewing cards, through which a piece of yarn is laced, enhances a child's motor skills and teaches the fundamentals of sewing. Yeah, sewing cards are a whole fucking lot of fun.

- If one of your children is killed playing with a chemistry set, make a game of it by challenging your surviving children to reanimate him or her.

- Visit your local mall for such upscale toy stores as Wooden Toys Your Kids Will Hate and Professor Faggot Q. Boredom's Lame-U-Cational Cocksuckery.

- One of the best educational toys you can buy your child is a pet. A rabbit, for example, can teach him or her about the life cycle, mammalian reproduction, toxicology, comparative anatomy, and cooking.

- When toy shopping, look for the Joe Mantegna Seal Of Safety. It's your only guarantee that the toy has been deemed safe by Joe Mantegna.

- Rounded edges on toys should be sharpened in case your child tries to chop vegetables with them.

- It's amazing how much kids can learn about chemistry the old-fashioned way. As soon as you get home from work, demand that they mix you an Old-Fashioned.

- After your child unwraps his or her new toy, throw it on the ground and stomp on it. If any small pieces break off, the toy is too dangerous for young children.

- Erector sets are a great way to get your preteen started on making juvenile sex puns.

- Buy your child expensive, collectible toys and forbid him or her to take them out of the box. This will teach your child valuable life lessons about longing, deprivation, and resentment.

World's Jews Celebrate Christmas With Ceremonial Re-Murdering Of Christ

JERUSALEM—As Christians everywhere celebrate the birth of Christ this holiday season, the world's approximately 14 million Jews are also commemorating the special holiday, as they do each year, by ceremonially re-murdering the Baby Jesus. Details of the time-honored Jewish tradition include the baking of a baby-shaped potato pancake, which is filled with beet juice and then beheaded by a demon-horned rabbi using a specially blessed "baby-killing" knife. "I love devouring Christians' young almost as much as corrupting maidens," said Benjamin Levy, 89. "It's a magical time for all." The re-murdering is among the most important celebrations of the Jewish calendar, second only to the springtime "Poisoning of the Easter Wells" festival.

Chicago Rolls Out Cold-Weather Prostitutes

CHICAGO—From the barren tree branches to the colorful Christmas decorations, the signs of another Windy City winter are everywhere you look. And with the chilly air and fresh snow comes the sight of local residents replacing their regular three-season hookers with prostitutes better capable of handling the tough Chicago streets.

Unlike many other parts of the country, where milder temperatures and lighter snowfalls allow for the convenience of all-year prostitutes, citizens of Chicago must turn to thicker, sturdier working girls who can provide the high performance needed to get through the worst their notorious winter has to offer.

"When temperatures drop below zero, you need prostitutes you can depend on when they're needed most," said area resident Phillip Eadie, who mounted four cold-weather hookers earlier this month. "The last thing you want during a raging blizzard is to get stuck with a prostitute who's not up to the task when it really counts."

"Seriously, if it weren't for cold-weather prostitutes, I don't think I'd ever leave the house," he added.

More resistant to heavy wear and tear than ordinary street whores, these high-performance prostitutes provide Chicago residents with optimal handling under the roughest of conditions, a firmer grip on ultra-slick surfaces, as well as greater rear-end balance. In addition to improved

Across the city, residents are swapping out regular hookers with more dedicated, cold-weather prostitutes in their cars.

start and stop capabilities, the prostitutes are also able to absorb the bumpiest of rides.

"I'm the kind of guy who likes to feel in control at all times, and cold-weather prostitutes give me just that," said resident Charles Wentel, adding that he was first turned on to the seasonal whores by his father. "With other prostitutes I would always worry about how they'd react to unpredictable situations or whether they had the flexibility necessary to take on any and all jobs."

> ## "More resistant to heavy wear and tear than ordinary street whores, these high-performance prostitutes provide Chicago residents with optimal handling under the roughest of conditions."

"I've shelled out a lot of money for a lot of hookers in my life, and let me tell you these cold-weather babies are by far the best," Wentel added. "You won't find me riding around with anything less this winter."

According to local dealers and distributors of winter-ready prostitutes, most summer hookers "have very little life left in them" by Thanksgiving and can "hardly be trusted" to manage street corners through the winter.

"You can rotate your old whores, tie them up in chains, dress them up any and each way you like, but it won't make a bit of a difference," said Dale Huza, who peddles cold-weather prostitutes in nine different downtown locations. "Since getting in the business five years ago, I've yet to hear of a single customer who's been let down by these hookers. Hell, I even use them myself."

Often selected as among the safest whores on the market, cold-weather prostitutes are also a popular choice for those who have families to think about.

"As a husband and father of two boys, I demand a lot from my call girls," said Henry Greenman, who admitted to having an easier time sleeping at night since picking up some cold-weather prostitutes. "After all, there's no way I can be taking risks with unsafe tramps knowing the effect they could have on my family."

"Sure they may cost a little more, but as I've always said, you can't put a price on peace of mind," he added.

Many members of the Chicago business community have come out in favor of cold-weather prostitutes.

Managers, employees, and two custodians at South Side Automotive strongly recommend the hookers this season, claiming that in a series of "side-by-side" tests conducted behind their premises, cold-weather prostitutes outperformed regular prostitutes in every winter trial.

"More than any other prostitutes we've come across, there's nothing these hookers can't and won't withstand, no environment you can put them in where they won't do what's required of them," owner Mike Watlak said. "I give cold-weather prostitutes my and my company's personal stamp of approval." ∅

Rommel, Hummel Dominate Parents' Christmas List

Biden Winks After Offering To Buy Eggnog For White House Christmas Party

WASHINGTON—During an unexpected visit Thursday to an organizational meeting for this year's White House Christmas party, Vice President Joe Biden winked mischievously as he offered to "handle" the eggnog supply for the upcoming annual event. "Uncle Joe's got the nog under control," said Biden, briefly flashing a metal flask protruding from the inside pocket of his suit jacket. "Old family recipe." Biden's appearance among White House event planners was his first since last May, when he offered to procure "some real fireworks" for the upcoming Fourth of July festivities.

Holiday Time Means Time For The Holiday Movies Time

The Silver Screen by Archie "Arch" Danielson

Jingle your bells over to the bijou, because it is now the holiday season that is the season when we have Christmas and the other holidays that so many families enjoy while spending time together in reverence and watching movies on the Silver Screen.

And because it is the holidays, I thought I would take a moment to reflect on some of the great holiday movies of days past and talk about the bad holiday movies of today, which are not very good. Merry Christmas!

I went to see a movie called *The Jingle Way Man* that is about a man who must go shopping for a toy because he wishes to spread some holiday cheer to his young son. (I do not have any children of my own, but I have spent many a year buying a present for my nephew Kenneth, who is now 27 and never comes over, even when I call him and tell him the gutter is full of garbage.) And in this movie the man was of foreign heritage. He spoke with a heavy accent and carried himself in a most amusing manner because he kept falling over into the fountain, and once he even dropped a bunch of packages onto a broad's head and broke her hat.

There was also a mailman in the film who was chasing the man, and they both made jackasses of themselves. Although maybe that was a different movie. In conclusion, there are better movies to see than *Jingling To The Mall* this holiday season.

When I was a young man of 24 (that was many years ago!) I used to go shopping in the downtown area of our city, and there were tiny elves in store windows, and the lights, oh, how they sparkled in the night and people would ring bells that made the air sound like it was full of ringing bells!

Then there was the Christmas season when I first started courting the ladies. Ah, I remember it as if it were only a few years ago. For example, there was the one woman named Clandice whose brother was a roustabout at the local carnival. But the carnival was closed during the holidays, and that was just fine with me and Clandice because it was too cold to take a spin on the ferris wheel, anyhow. So Clandice and I would walk down to the lake where men of character could be seen ice fishing, and then once I caught her under the mistletoe and gave her a smooch right in her bathroom!

> **"Toots cannot find our Christmas decorations, and I think it is because she accidentally gave them to a vagrant who said he was from the Salvation Army. Where does the time go?"**

Those were the days! And we would go to holiday movies that would make you happy to be watching, such as *The Nuns And The Bells*, which was about some women who ran a school and they were dressed as nuns, I think because they were nuns. And these women taught the boys to box and to always remember their school.

Why do no children today have the school spirit? I was proud to attend Beaver Dam High School, though I did not go to college because I was anxious to join the service and see the sights. Then in the movie it was Christmas Eve, and one little girl didn't have any parents except for a mother. And her mother was a common harlot, so the girl did bad on a test, and they kicked her out of school. I do not remember how *The Bells And The Nuns* ended, except I hope it had a happy ending because thinking of that girl now is bringing a frown to my face, and I do not want to be sad during the holidays.

> ## "At the end of the movie everyone is happy because it is snowing and everyone is drunk. They do not make movies like that anymore. We used to call them 'moving film' in those days, because they were moving pictures."

Another movie that is good to watch while you have your family gathered around the hearth (although it is not good to watch movies on the television. I much prefer seeing them in a movie theater where you are allowed to smoke a cigar during the picture, because my wife Toots does not let me smoke cigars in the house. I used to frequent a particular theater which was at that time called The Orpheus, and they would have candied delights for one and all. But you had to pay for them. Some things never change!)

What was I saying before? Oh, yes. Another good holiday movie is called *The Wonderful Life Of Mr. Smith*, and it is about a man who wants to jump off a bridge, but he instead decides to go to Washington (our nation's capital city) to become a senator, and then an angel comes down and steals some money, and there is also a scene where a druggist slaps the ear of a young boy. And a cop fires a gun, which is rather violent! Anyway, at the end of the movie everyone is happy because it is snowing and everyone is drunk. They do not make movies like that anymore. We used to call them "moving film" in those days, because they were moving pictures.

I hope that my nephew Kenneth will come to visit me this Christmas, although I don't think he will because last year I told his mother that her hair looked like a dirty old rat. Toots will not let me drink nog of egg this year for that reason. But I do not blame her. I hung a wreath on the door and it looks rather festive.

Happy holidays from the Silver Screen! And ho, ho, ho! And watch some holiday movies that I have mentioned if they come to your town. Toots cannot find our Christmas decorations, and I think it is because she accidentally gave them to a vagrant who said he was from the Salvation Army. Where does the time go?

Mr. Danielson's column is reprinted from The Butternut Gazette *in Butternut, OH. It has been edited for the sake of clarity.* ✐

Hanukkah Decorations Being Defaced Earlier Every Year

NEW YORK—A report released Monday by the Anti-Defamation League confirmed the widely held perception that Hanukkah decorations are being vandalized earlier every season. "Today, we're seeing Stars of David spray-painted with swastikas before the leaves have even fallen," said ADL spokesman Avi Mendenhall. "Our research shows that, even as recently as a decade ago, a menorah wouldn't be toppled over until well after Thanksgiving." The report noted that many shopping malls have, in recent years, begun playing anti-Semitic carols just days after Halloween.

Rove Implicated In Santa Identity Leak

WASHINGTON, DC—The recent leak revealing Santa Claus to be "your mommy and daddy" has been linked to President Bush's senior political adviser and deputy chief of staff Karl Rove.

"If this devastating leak, which severely undermines the security of children everywhere and has compromised parent-child relations, came from the highest levels of the White House, that is an outrage," said former Bush counterterrorism adviser and outspoken Bush Administration critic Richard Clarke.

The identity of the mythical holiday gift-giver, previously known only in grown-up circles, was published in the popular *Timbertoes* cartoon in the December issue of *Highlights For Children*. Jean Abrams, a conservative firebrand known to have close ties to Bush appointees in the Department of Education, revealed "Santa" to be a code name for anonymous parental gift-giving.

Abrams and several other children's-magazine journalists, including *Ranger Rick*'s Kristin Brittany and *Cricket* managing editor Shaina Belowitz, have testified before a federal grand jury on the source of the leak. Sources say that Randall Polk, Washington bureau chief for *Weekly Reader,* named Rove after serving eight days in jail for refusing to divulge his sources.

Federal investigators began to suspect a White House connection to the Santa leak when Abrams wrote in *Timbertoes* that the character of Pa had some "devastating information" on "very high authority."

"Did you know that Santa Claus is really just your mommy and daddy?" Pa's dialogue read. "It's true. Sometimes parents tell little white lies to their children to make them feel special."

Clarke criticized the leak as "foolhardy," saying it was "the kind of conduct you would expect from dangerous zealots who routinely confuse short-term political gain with the national interest."

"This leak compromises generations of undercover work on the part of U.S. parents," Clarke said. "Consider all the covers that will be blown, all the secret gift-hiding places that will be exposed."

The motivations behind the leak remain unclear, but some political observers have characterized it as a calculated act of retribution against Fairfax, VA, second-grader Madison Harris. Harris, 7, wore an antiwar T-shirt to her elementary school during a Nov. 2 visit by Education Secretary Margaret Spellings.

> **"'I don't consider it precocious to wear peace T-shirts and, from what I hear, read *Highlights*.'"**

"The shirt, decorated with doves and the word 'peace,' angered White House ideologues, who felt that Harris had undermined a tightly orchestrated visit," independent political media watchdog Ellen Applebee said. "An aggressive attempt to hit Harris where she lived was set in motion."

On Nov. 3, Rove told reporters, "People shouldn't take too seriously the opinions of someone who still thinks a fat man slides down the chimney into her living room every December 25." On Nov. 6, he told several aides, "I don't consider it precocious to wear peace T-shirts and, from what I hear, read *Highlights*."

Applebee cited these comments as

evidence of "Rove's deliberate campaign against Harris."

During that same week, Rove is also believed to have placed calls to several of the children's-magazine journalists who were later called before the grand jury.

If Rove is responsible for leaking Santa's identity to the world's children, it would not be his first political "dirty trick." In 1988, he was fired from George H. W. Bush's presidential campaign for sending an unsigned letter to the young daughter of a Dukakis campaign adviser. In the let-ter, he revealed the sad ending of the film *Old Yeller*.

On Capitol Hill, many say they believe that the damage has already been done. Clarke cited the absence of Santas from several department stores across the country as possible evidence that their compromised identities fatally damaged their credibility.

"I don't envy parents of young children right now," Clarke said. "Trust has been shattered. I wouldn't be surprised if some moms and dads are forced into hiding." ⌀

Attempt To Buy Gift For Boyfriend Results In Hatred Of Boyfriend

SIERRA VISTA, AZ—After a week spent searching for the perfect Christmas gift for Jed Lowry, her boyfriend of eight months, Susan Novecky realized that she, in fact, despises him. "I tried to find a book he might like, but now that I think about it, the only reading materials I've ever seen in his apartment are old issues of *Maxim* and Dennis Miller's *The Rants*," Novecky said. "Then I thought I'd use the gift as an opportunity to fix one of his flaws, but why bother buying cologne for someone who doesn't even own a decent pair of goddamn pants?" When Novecky decided to just call Lowry and ask him what he wanted, Lowry said he needed a new Xbox controller because he spilled beer all over the other one.

How Are We Losing Holiday Weight?

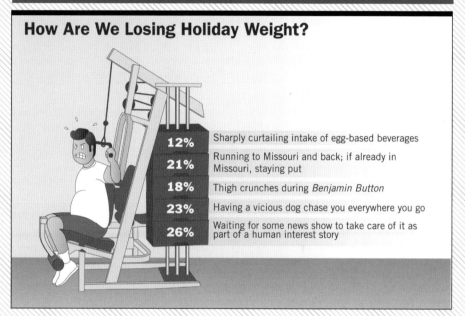

12% Sharply curtailing intake of egg-based beverages

21% Running to Missouri and back; if already in Missouri, staying put

18% Thigh crunches during *Benjamin Button*

23% Having a vicious dog chase you everywhere you go

26% Waiting for some news show to take care of it as part of a human interest story

Non-Widescreen Version Of DVD Received As Hanukkah Gift

BROOKLYN, NY—Self-described film buff Tyler Rosenstein was disappointed to receive a non-letterboxed "full screen" version of the movie *The Matrix Reloaded* as a Hanukkah gift, the 19-year-old reported Monday.

"Great," said Rosenstein, concealing his displeasure from his beaming aunt and uncle, Hannah and Bernie Greenberg, as he gazed at the freshly unwrapped DVD in his hand. "Just what I wanted. *The Matrix Reloaded*."

"With approximately a third of the movie's visual content missing, thanks to 'pan-and-scan,'" he added under his breath.

Rosenstein, a freshman studying philosophy at NYU, said he was momentarily excited to receive the special collector's edition DVD of *The Matrix Reloaded*, which features more than an hour of supplemental material, including behind-the-scenes footage and a preview of the *Enter The Matrix* video game. But Rosenstein's joy faded when his eye caught the words "full-screen edition" emblazoned across the top of the box.

Minutes later, Rosenstein's cousin Cory made an exchange of the gift impossible

Rosenstein holds the inadequate gift.

when he insisted that Rosenstein open the DVD to show him the "easter egg."

While Rosenstein thanked his aunt and uncle for the gift, he took leave of the family get-together shortly after dinner and locked himself in his room to sulk.

"'Why would they even release a full-screen *Matrix Reoladed*, when every single frame of that movie is so artfully composed?'"

"It's frustrating, because they came so close to getting me exactly what I wanted," said Rosenstein, lying on his bed and sneering at the DVD. "This is a $30 item. But what am I supposed to do with it? Why would they even release a full-screen *Matrix Reloaded*, when every single frame of that movie is so artfully composed? Even leaving framing aside, the movie cries out for each of its visual elements to be seen."

"It's an unwatchable piece of crap," said Rosenstein, tossing the DVD onto a pile of gifts that included a sweatshirt and a digital memo recorder.

In spite of his annoyance with the non-letterboxed DVD, Rosenstein said he knew better than to complain to his relatives.

"There's just no way to tell them without coming off like a complete asshole," Rosenstein said. "I'm just going to have to eat it."

The Greenbergs remain unaware of their mistake.

"We're so happy that we were able to get Tyler a gift he really wanted this year," Hannah Greenberg said. "You wouldn't believe how hard he is to shop for. He's so picky about his movies. For his birthday, we gave him *The Wedding Singer*. I thought all the kids liked that Adam Sandler—Cory said

he sings a song about Hanukkah. Well, boy, was getting Tyler that movie a mistake!"

This year, instead of guessing, the Greenbergs took a suggestion from Rosenstein's father, who was aware that his son owned the first *Matrix* movie.

"Tyler's got very specific tastes," Bernie said. "He told us he likes those foreign films. What did he call it? The Criterion Collection. Well, Hannah and I tried to find those, but they didn't have them at Target. We sure didn't want what happened with the wizard movie to happen again."

Bernie spoke in reference to last year, when the Greenbergs came close to finding a gift Rosenstein would like. The misguided couple gave their nephew the theatrical-release version of *Lord Of The Rings: The Fellowship Of The Ring*, instead of the extended version which contains 40 extra minutes of footage—a distinction Rosenstein gently explained to the confused gift-givers.

"If we'd known, we'd have been happy to get him the other version," Hannah said. "Well, this time we were very careful. There were two versions at the store, and we made sure to get the special one. See, Tyler hates it when they cut out part of the movie."

Confusion over the misleading term "full-screen" caused his well-meaning relatives to purchase the inferior version of the DVD.

"Why do they call it 'full-screen' anyway, when it's only two-thirds of the stupid movie?" Rosenstein asked. "Fucking bullshit aspect ratio!"

As of press time, Rosenstein had not decided what to do with the DVD.

"I can't trade it to any of my friends," Rosenstein said. "They'd just roll their eyes when they saw it wasn't letterboxed. Basically, I'm screwed. I'm stuck with a product that has no reason to exist."

"I suppose I could just throw it away," Rosenstein continued. "But what if Aunt Hannah or Uncle Bernie asked about it? I'll probably have to just keep this horrible thing on my shelf. I'm trapped, like Neo and the other warriors of Zion, in a fictitious world I never chose to be a part of: an imaginary alternate universe where non-widescreen DVDs are remotely tolerable." ✐

Santa Signs Legislation To Help Special-Wants Children

NORTH POLE—Kristofer Kringle, an international toy distributor popularly known as "Santa Claus," approved elf-penned legislation Monday that grants greater benefits to often-neglected "special wants" children. "Old policies failed to reward the world's children for dreaming big, but no longer—children with special or unusual wants shall see them all fulfilled on Christmas morning," Kringle said, in an announcement met with strong support from parents of the developmentally entitled. "My children were all born with special wants," said Glenda Froman, mother of three. "After years of whiny suffering, they'll finally have their wish: Xbox 360s in every room, matching ponies, and a rocket-powered bicycle they're allowed to fly inside the house."

Wah, Wah, I Have Seasonal Affective Disorder

Hey, everybody, look at me, I'm a tiny little baby who lets winter cold and an hour or two of extra darkness keep me from functioning. Boo-hoo, I've got seasonal affective disorder. All I feel like doing is sitting in my apartment, eating, and going beddy-bye because my hypothalamus can't cope with the decreased amount of daylight.

By Sharon Marcus

Boo-hoo, I have fewer melanopsin proteins than regular people.

Poor me, every morning I have trouble getting out of bed because it's still dark outside when I leave for work. The gray clouds and the icy slush and the brutal cold and ever-present darkness remind me of my impending doom. They magnify all my latent fears and feelings of hopelessness. Whine!

I never feel this way when Mr. Sun is shining with all his might. I wish I could slumber all winter like a bear and not even be aware of the gloomy old winter outside and wake up in April when the grass is growing and the trees are budding and the flowers are blooming. Or better yet, I wish I could live in a magical place where it's sunny and warm all year round. Then I could be happy and have fun. But, wah, I can't afford to move, so I'm forced to live in dumb old Des Moines, where the sun dies at 4:49 p.m.

Blubber-blub-blub, I've lost my social and intellectual coping mechanisms necessary to maintain my mental well-being, all because of a neurological condition over which I have no control and was afflicted with by a cruel random accident of biology. Pity poor little me! Every day between January and March is a living nightmare because I'm more psychologically vulnerable to the seasonal tilting of the planetary axis than most people—wah, wah, wah!

Well, at least I have my $300 dawn simulator. As mean Old Man Dark approaches, I stare at it for 30 whole minutes and hope that its bright artificial light will cheer me up. But boo-hoo-hoo, my serotonin levels still aren't increasing. Besides, a dawn simulator is no substitute for wonderful, glorious Mr. Sun.

Where are you, Mr. Sun? I thought you were my friend!

Boo-hoo, I'm just a self-pitying little baby with a clinically diagnosed disorder who just wants to cry all the time or stare into space. My family doesn't understand me. They don't know why I just can't pull myself together. They think I'm crazy when they catch me gazing numbly at the kitchen wall. Sob! I am unable to pick up my 3-year-old and hug her or feel any motherly joy because I lack the sufficient amount of rods and cones in my retinas.

> ## "Boo-hoo, I have fewer melanopsin proteins than regular people."

Wahhh! Will Mr. Sun ever come out again? What if he never does? Oh, no! See, because I have seasonal affective disorder, I think about stuff like this all the time. That, and suicide!

Just because it was cloudy outside yesterday, I had a big old panic attack and had to go to the hospital. My husband had to pick me up from the emergency room, and boy was he mad. I think everybody hates me! I feel totally worthless, and that makes my seasonal affective disorder worse! Bawl!

Well, March 21 can't come fast enough. That's the first day of spring! On that day, my energy levels will magically increase because Mr. Sun is positioned above the equator. Soon the days will be longer and the sunlight shinier, and I can finally raise the shades in my bedroom and have friends again and sing and dance and play. I have the date circled on my calendar with a big smiley face saying, "Rise and shine, Sharon! It's spring! Mr. Sun is going to hug you today. You're allowed to laugh for the first time in three whole months!" It'll be the bestest day ever.

But it's still over a month away! And I can't do anything about it but curl up under the covers praying for relief to a cruel God who probably doesn't even exist. Boo-hoo-hoo-hoo-hoo! Poor, poor me! *

Quick, Painless Death Tops Holiday Wish List Of Local Veal Calf

BUTLER, OH—A four-month-old veal calf revealed Monday that topping its Christmas list this year is a quick, painless death. "I would like the end to come soon," said the calf, speaking from its one-by-two-foot pen. "And when it does come, I hope it is not agonizing." Sources close to the calf were surprised that more spacious living quarters and a longer life did not come higher on its list, coming in three and six, respectively. Number two on the calf's list was a Panasonic wet/dry razor.

Powerful Rest And Fluids Industry Influencing Doctors' Treatment of Colds

WASHINGTON—A two-year investigation conducted in five major cities has exposed a widespread campaign by the formidable Rest and Fluids industry to infiltrate thousands of doctors' offices and dictate how they treat minor illnesses.

The investigation—the full details of which will be disclosed in this newspaper over the coming months—documented thousands of instances in which sick patients were repeatedly instructed, often verbatim, to "lie down and drink plenty of liquids." This treatment, recommended a staggering 4 out of 5 times on average, was in each case prescribed by a physician known to have recently enjoyed a golf vacation courtesy of Big Rest and Fluids.

"You have no idea how deep this goes," said Dr. X, a physician who wished to remain anonymous. "They've got everyone, from the pediatricians and family doctors, right on down to the school nurses. We've

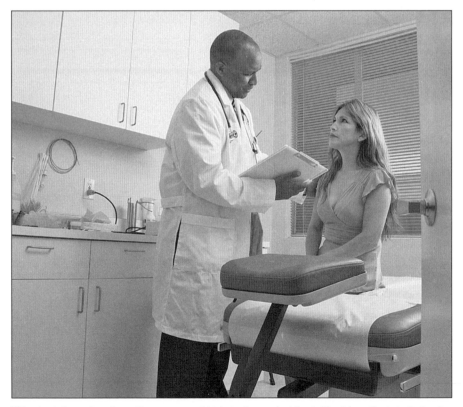

This physician enjoyed an all-expenses-paid trip to Aspen, just for telling his patients to "relax."

had the cure for the common cold for nearly 40 years, but it's still 'rest and fluids, rest and fluids.' Why? Because these guys are getting paid through the nose, that's why."

> ## "What began as a small-scale racket has today grown into a multinational organization, with billions of dollars devoted each year to pushing its pro-napping, broth-focused agenda."

"The complimentary king-sized beds, the downy soft comforters, the absolutely ravishing women," Dr. X continued. "It's a sick, sick world."

The American Rest and Fluids industry first rose to prominence during the Great Influenza Pandemic of 1918, when there existed only meager competition from quarantines and prayer. After gaining influence during the '20s and '30s, mainly through mob connections and a few corrupt U.S. senators, R&F was again buoyed in 1947 following the introduction of employee sick days.

What began as a small-scale racket has today grown into a multinational organization, with billions of dollars devoted each year to pushing its pro-napping, broth-focused agenda.

"At this point, it may be impossible to unseat the power Rest and Fluids has over the American health system," patients rights activist Oren Michem said. "With

their promises of free La-Z-Boy chairs and high-priced hotel rooms, it's no wonder they've cornered the cold market. Sure, they never come out and ask, 'Can Rest and Fluids count on your loyalty?' But the intention is obvious."

"It took my son nearly a week to stop sneezing and coughing," Michem added. "Who's to say a regimen of strenuous exercise and fasting wouldn't have helped him more?"

To date, no doctors have been willing to testify against these so-called Rest and Fluids "fat cats" for fear it would destroy their careers. In fact, a number of physicians have already been blackballed for prescribing echinacea and other over-the-counter remedies.

Worse yet, some fear violent retribution for not toeing the Rest and Fluids line. In 1997, four Chicago doctors who were known to prescribe cough syrup were found dead at the bottom of a pool of Ny-Quil. Officially, these deaths were blamed on the less-powerful Natural Causes industry, but many still believe the message delivered that day was clear.

Representatives of Rest and Fluids have refused to comment on the allegations.

"My clients have nothing to say about this or any other litigation involving R&F," said Robert Marconi, one of the industry's legion of high-paid defense attorneys. "Rest and Fluids has done nothing wrong and will fight these charges for as long as it takes. They can't prove a thing!"

With a recent $12.3 million donation to several prominent Washington bureaucrats, Rest and Fluids will most likely continue its stranglehold for decades to come. That is, unless one young and energetic nurse practitioner from Louisiana has his say.

This newspaper has recently learned that whistle-blower Nathan Bellows has collected a mountain of evidence outlining years of blackmail and corruption on the part of R&F. Evidence, Bellows said, he plans to leak to 12 major media outlets later this week.

Bellows lives at 138 Juniper St., Apt. 3H, Folsom, LA, 70437. He goes jogging every morning around the nearby reservoir and is always alone. ✐

Shitty Human Being Blames Decreased Daylight This Time

CEDAR RAPIDS, IA—Horrible person James MacDougal, an account executive at the properties management firm Gordon, Olster and French, this time blamed his constant shitty behavior toward others on the shortened days of the fall season, sources reported Monday. "The lack of sunlight makes me cranky," said MacDougal, who in previous months has blamed the humidity, his favorite sports team losing, not getting enough sleep, and the "terrible" office coffee for making him a total, unrelenting asshole. "I've snapped at [secretary] Lynette three times this week. I should really apologize. It's just my knee has been killing me lately." By midwinter, MacDougal is expected by coworkers to revert to such time-tested excuses as having to change to snow tires, being "under the weather," and the annual Christmas visit from "[his] griping bitch of a mom."

Ghost Of Christmas Future Taunts Children With Visions Of PlayStation 5

SOUTHFIELD, MI—Bored with scaring elderly misers, the Ghost of Christmas Future is spending the holiday season taunting modern children with visions of Christmas 2016's hottest toy: the Sony PlayStation 5, a 2,048-bit console featuring a 45-Ghz trinary processor, CineReal graphics booster with 2-gig biotexturing, and an RSP connector for 360-degree on-line-immersion play.

"You know how kids are—a year is an eternity to them," the wraithlike specter said Monday during a visit to the Southfield home of 13-year-old Josh Kuehn. "So just imagine showing them something they'll have to wait 14 years for. Teasing them with a glimpse of the PS5 is the ultimate torture. They absolutely lose their minds.

It's like saying, 'Hey, kid, you'll be an old man before you ever get to touch this.'"

The Ghost of Christmas Future said he has visited more than 125,000 homes since Thanksgiving, offering children an agonizing sneak peek at what they cannot have for another decade and a half.

"I like to appear in the living room with a PS5 hooked up to 2016's most popular TV, the 4'x8' Hi-Def Sony Titania," the Ghost said. "Then, I'll say in my best spooky voice, 'Jimmy! Behold what your kids will be playing while you're slaving away at an office job to support them!'"

Driving the children mad with PS5 lust, the Ghost said, is a multi-step process.

"I usually start by showing them Toteki Aluminum, one of the future's most popular

The Ghost of Christmas Future offers a pair of Phoenix 10-year-olds a tantalizing glimpse of the PS5.

fight-and-chase games," the Ghost said. "It's far from the best available in 2016, but it always blows their mind to see the guy get hit with the falling sign while the drops of sweat fly off his face. You can see the whole scene, distorted, in each of the individual drops. That gives them a good preliminary idea of the graphics technology we're dealing with."

The Ghost said he then likes to show Airsledz, a racing game in which jet-powered sleds whoosh through a four-dimensional racing course in the sky. The game, he said, enables the player to compete online against dozens of other players all around the world.

> ## "'That's when I go in for the kill by casually mentioning that the game comes packaged with the 2016 feature film of the same name—not on DVD, of course, but on SCAP. Ten times better.'"

"They always ask if you can play it on the Internet—it's so cute how they still call it 'the Internet'—and I tell them, 'Hey, you can play this against 63 other PS5 owners simultaneously. At least you can in 14 years,'" the Ghost said. "And you should see their jaws hit the floor when they learn about the add-on accessories that enable users to actually fly around the room during gameplay."

Once the capabilities of the system are conveyed to the children, the Ghost likes to push them further over the edge by showing them games specially targeted to their age group.

Younger children, he said, salivate upon seeing Level One of Zonic Fugue. In it, Zonic, the indigo-colored son of Sonic The Hedgehog, faces off against Chuckles The Echidna in a Terrordactyl sky-joust, attempting to earn the Ankle Rockets he needs to gather the five Chaos Sapphires that, when combined, form the master key that opens the Melody Dome.

To break the spirits of children 12 and up, the Ghost runs a brief demonstration of Back To Werewolf Island. The horror-action thriller, he said, will be produced in full 10.8 Omneo sound and feature new music from 40 of 2016's hottest skagcore acts, including FU3P, Dredgerous, and Frances Cobain.

"Sometimes, the kids will start getting defensive and say, 'Yeah, well, I don't know any of those characters, so big deal,'" the Ghost said. "That's when I pull out DC vs. Marvel."

The Ghost said he shows the children a brief clip of DC vs. Marvel, in which cinema-realistic figures of Spider-Man and the Joker dash across impossibly detailed city streets, attacking each other with dozens of different offensive maneuvers while leaping, somersaulting, and throwing objects.

"They usually start trembling at that point," the Ghost said. "That's when I go in for the kill by casually mentioning that the game comes packaged with the 2016 feature film of the same name—not on DVD, of course, but on SCAP. Ten times better."

The few children unbroken by DC vs. Marvel are invariably finished off by the sight of Star Wars—Episode IX: Jedi Destiny, a game which employs the world's most advanced artificial-intelligence algorithm to place the player inside the film's climactic battle sequence on the planet Mon Jeedam.

"With more than 12,000 distinct soldiers, creatures, and vehicles fighting at once, and the option to command the New Republic Fleet, the Imperial Armada, or the Yuuzhan Vong Invasion Force, it's not merely the best Star Wars game that's ever existed; it's an interactive film that looks better than any movie that's ever been made. No child has failed to sob hysterically at the sight of it."

The PlayStation 5 will be available in stores Nov. 12, 2016, at a list price of 399 New Dollars ($199 Canadian). ∅

Cold And Flu Prevention Tips

Here are some tips to help keep you healthy and germ-free during these cold winter months:

- Sneezing into a handkerchief just redirects germs back at you. Always sneeze outward so as to shoot germs as far across the room as possible.

- Pack your sinus cavities with Vicks Vap-O-Rub to fully mentholate your respiratory system.

- Do not blow your stuffed nose into tissues—this is a myth! Always suck your phlegm into the back of your throat and swallow it in great, goblike mouthfuls.

- You don't have to subject yourself to other people's germs. If you see someone who appears to have a cold or fever, contact your local police department.

- To prevent infections, have sick people cough into your food. This light "inoculative" dose of germs will boost your body's defenses against a full-blown infection later.

- If you are a sickly, anemic, weak person, you have a higher susceptibility to colds and flu. Try not to be such a pansy-ass.

- Sometimes, a severe respiratory infection will cause the lungs to fill with fluid. If this occurs, flush your lungs repeatedly with boiling hot water to clear them. A hose down your windpipe will help get around the gag reflex.

- Make sure your HMO package covers visits to the Halls Of Medicine.

- The flu is an extremely contagious, life-threatening disease. Flu sufferers should be either shot with a silver bullet or tortured to death by a professionally shriven, church-appointed excruciator.

- To keep warm in the winter, replace your blood with mom's homemade chicken soup. Noodles should be no greater than one millimeter thick to prevent coronary blockage.

- Remember: Your body produces phlegm for a reason. Always save your mucous, and keep it near you in jars at all times.

- Germs generally enter the body through the skin. To protect you from infection, shave yours off.

- Zinc and Vitamin C help fight colds. Vitamin C can be found in oranges, but zinc is a semi-precious metal found only in Africa. If symptoms persist, organize a jungle safari to seek out the fabled Zinc Mines of Sugolahara.

Department-Store Santa Told To Push Chinaware

UTICA, NY—Art Schultz, better known as the Senpike Mall's Santa Claus, carried out the management-issued directive to push fine china dinnerware during dozens of two-minute lap sessions Monday. "Ho, ho, ho! Has Bobby been a good boy this year so Santa can bring him, a, uh, Wedgwood five-piece bone china setting in the timeless 'Crown Gold' pattern?" Schultz said to perplexed 5-year-old Robert Ullings. "Maybe if you're on your best behavior, and a big help to Mommy, Santa could bring you...a Lenox gravy boat!" Schultz bolstered his holiday messages by urging children to act now, as their good behavior could qualify their parents for a 10 percent discount on their first Nordstrom credit-card purchase.

Feds Uncover Secret Santa Ring

BLOOMINGTON, IN—The FBI arrested 34 people and seized $157 in small, tasteful presents Monday in what is believed to be the largest bust of a Secret Santa ring in U.S. history.

The ring's base of operations, FBI director Louis Freeh said, was Creative Concepts, a Bloomington-area marketing firm. According to Freeh, all of the ring's participants were employees of Creative Concepts, mostly working in the secretarial pool and mail room, with a few coming from the client-services and accounting departments.

"It took nearly two years to secure sufficient hard evidence and eyewitness testimony, but we feel we have a solid case against them," said Freeh following the raid. "We believe that this Secret Santa ring had been operating at Creative Concepts for upwards of 15 years, and that thousands of gifts, from Dilbert coffee mugs to giant Hershey kisses, had been exchanged during that period of time. We are hopeful that the reign of Yuletide graft and corruption that has infested this company for so long has finally come to an end."

Among the items seized in the raid were three Sheaffer ballpoint pens, a bag of Jelly Belly jelly beans, two poinsettia plants, an Indianapolis Colts Christmas-tree ornament, a box of Ferrero Rocher bon bons, a Mannheim Steamroller CD, a 4"x6" silver picture frame, a Mooch The Monkey Beanie Baby, a pair of mittens, a *Dorf On Golf* video and several items believed to have originated from a mall-based Successories store.

Despite the success of Monday's raid, much about Secret Santa operations remains unknown. It is generally accepted by criminologists that Secret Santaism is a seasonal practice taking place exclusively around Christmastime, and involves the exchange of gifts, usually costing no more than $10 each.

According to Lester Long, a freelance criminal profiler and analyst, cracking a Secret Santa ring is difficult, because "the key to Secret Santaism is anonymity."

"The ring members commence their operations by writing their names on small scraps of paper, then surreptitiously placing the scraps in a hat or a small bucket or tin," Long said. "Then, each member quietly draws a single name and does not divulge who this person is to anyone. Nor does this member know who drew out his or her own name. Everyone is sworn to total silence and secrecy. This means participants are able to cover their tracks and protect each other's identity."

Added Long: "That's why it's so hard to run surveillance on suspected Secret Santa ring members when they go shopping—for all we know, they could be buying gifts for family members or friends. So possible civil-rights violations come into play. It's ingenious, really."

> "'Everyone is sworn to total silence and secrecy. This means participants are able to cover their tracks and protect each other's identity.'"

Sorely lacking in circumstantial evidence, law-enforcement officials have come to depend on information from informants and infiltrators planted in suspected Secret Santa rings. Much of what is known about these schemes comes from now-retired FBI agent Clayton "Hap" Roemer, who, posing as a claims adjustor, infiltrated a Secret Santa ring at a Freehold, NJ, insurance firm in the late 1960s.

Roemer detailed his experiences in his 1982 book *Santa's Secrets: My Harrowing Undercover Life In The Center Of An Office Yuletide Racket.*

"At times, work came to a virtual standstill as people chatted about the items they hoped to get on 'Secret Santa Day,' which normally coincided with the regular, perfectly legal office Christmas party," Roemer wrote. "A pair of white gloves for church? A Harold Robbins novel? Anything was possible for a Secret Santa, provided it was under the agreed monetary limit.

Roemer's work resulted in the arrest of 22 people and the eventual dismantling of the Freehold office racket. But despite this and subsequent decades of similar efforts, Secret Santaism still thrives to this day.

"Today's Secret Santa participants are far more savvy than those of Agent Roemer's time," Long said. "For example,

they've learned not to post gift wish lists on the break-room board—that's an instant giveaway that Secret Santa activities are present. They also avoid using intra-office e-mail, which can be read by managerial higher-ups, and they assiduously destroy any evidence of a Secret Santa party, such as gift wrap, Dixie Cups and leftover poundcake."

Crime historians believe Secret Santa rings got their start among the office employees of a storage-and-transfer business in New York's Lower East Side in the late 1950s. From there, it slowly spread, finding its way into businesses throughout New England and the upper Midwest. By the mid-1970s, it had made its way to the burgeoning Sun Belt and the West Coast.

The accused members of the Creative Concepts Secret Santa ring are scheduled to appear before a federal magistrate on Jan. 15. They are charged with first-degree racketeering and improper expectation of gifts from professional colleagues. ✒

The Creative Concepts sales office that served as headquarters for the Secret Santa ring.

Fall Internship Pays Off With Coveted Winter Internship

NEW YORK—New York University student Dave Werner announced Monday that he has successfully parlayed an unpaid fall internship at the magazine *GQ* into a long-sought-after unpaid winter internship at the ESPN network. "After three months spent fetching coffee and making copies, all my hard work has finally paid off," the 21-year-old communications major said as he dropped off executive assistant Matt Sullivan's dry cleaning at a local laundromat. "These days, I'm totally in charge of taking lunch orders, and some of the people I work with already sort of know my name. What an invaluable experience." Werner added that his main goal is to use his connections at ESPN to secure a highly desirable spring internship that could possibly offer school credit and a modest travel stipend.

Grandma Concerned About Dinner Roll Count

ROCKFORD, IL—Local grandmother Eileen Stafford, 78, expressed concern Monday over the number of dinner rolls she should have on hand for this year's Christmas meal, appearing distressed when discussing the implications of there being either too many or possibly too few.

On a recent trip to the supermarket, Stafford reportedly purchased a package of 12 enriched white dinner rolls that was on sale for $1.89, and has since remained torn over whether a second package is necessary.

"They're a little small, and I don't want anyone to go hungry," said Stafford, carefully removing the rolls from the grocery bag to examine them more closely. "Of course, I can always give mine away if there's someone who doesn't get enough."

Added Stafford, "I don't have to have any rolls."

The elderly grandmother of four told reporters that, while she would hate for anything to go to waste, she would be equally upset if one of her guests reached into her wicker basket and found nothing but crumbs.

"Bill usually has two, even though he really shouldn't," said Stafford, referring to her son-in-law, whose above-average appetite she must always take into consideration when planning family meals. "And [daughter] Sheila's on that diet where they don't eat any bread."

Despite her insistence that she really doesn't want to bother anyone about anything, Stafford admitted that in the past week she has contacted several family members on multiple occasions to get an idea of how much company might be coming over.

Pacing nervously in her kitchen, the

An offer by Stafford's son to make an emergency supermarket trip if the rolls run out has done little to calm her fears.

small septuagenarian admitted that, even if she were to acquire an accurate estimate of those planning to attend, the number still could increase or decrease dramatically without any notice.

"Sandy doesn't make it home for holidays much since the divorce, but you never know," Stafford said of her youngest son. "And [grandson] Dennis sometimes gets called into work at the last minute, because he is a very good doctor and people trust him and rely on him. Still, it would be a real shame if that happened five Christmases in a row."

> ## "'It's just a turkey, for Christ's sake, and Dad isn't the one carving it anymore. I am. I'm the one carving the damn turkey now.'"

As a precautionary measure, Stafford has made several trips to nearby grocery stores to ensure that suitable dinner rolls are still available should a need for them arise in the coming days. If an emergency leaves her with no time to purchase an additional package, Stafford said she is prepared to defrost the hot dog buns in her freezer, a surplus from her upsetting overestimate of the turnout for this year's Memorial Day picnic.

According to a longtime friend who spoke with Stafford at church Sunday morning, the grandmother became flustered when discussing the possibility of someone bringing a girlfriend or boyfriend unannounced. Stafford, who lives alone in the house where she and her late husband raised their children, also said that she fears failure to serve her guests an appropriate amount of food might re-

sult in family members deciding to host next year's Christmas festivities at one of their own homes instead.

Eileen Stafford

"Grandma gets so worked up about the littlest stuff," said Amy Joyner, Stafford's granddaughter. "She's been calling me a couple times a day to update me on her dinner preparations and ask if I know about a better sale on sweet potatoes near us."

Joyner said since her grandfather Walter Stafford passed away in 2005, the holidays have made her grandmother uneasy because she worries that no one will be able to carve the turkey into "nice-sized" pieces the way Grandpa used to.

"It's always, 'Oh, no, that's not how Walter used to carve it—you should really carve it thicker, like your father would,'" said eldest son Michael Stafford, who has taken over many of the patriarchal duties in recent years. "It's just a turkey, for Christ's sake, and Dad isn't the one carving it anymore. I am. I'm the one carving the damn turkey now."

In addition to her roll-related anxieties, family sources reported that Stafford still has not decided whether to serve frozen or canned corn. ✐

2007 Holiday Cheer Brought To You By Toyota

NEW YORK—In one of the largest marketing coups in recent years, holiday cheer—the intangible spirit of goodwill towards man, peace on Earth, and warmth in the hearts of all—will now be sponsored by the Toyota Motor Corporation, sources reported Tuesday.

The exclusive $30 million deal, which includes promotional tie-ins with the season's first snowfall and the smell of roasted turkey wafting gently through a warm and cozy home, was signed earlier this week by Toyota Motor Sales U.S.A. executive vice president James Lentz.

"We are very excited to be working with holiday cheer," said Lentz, who called the look of wonder on a young child's face and the company's new line of durable trucks a "natural pairing." "From now on, whenever anyone curls up in front of a crackling fire-place, or takes a moment to reflect on the importance of family, Toyota will be there."

Added Lentz: "This truly is the most wonderful time of the year."

While many details of the deal are still unclear, Lentz said that the automotive company has been awarded endorsement rights to all affection and joy experienced during the month of December. Toyota will also be the chief sponsor of numerous holiday-related events, such as the untangling of Christmas lights while listening to Bing Crosby sing old seasonal classics, and the making or consuming of eggnog.

Additionally, as is specified in the terms of the agreement, all sugar plum fairies will now be preceded by a 15-second Toyota ad before dancing inside consumers' heads.

"Landing holiday cheer was huge for us," said Toyota marketing executive Rebecca

One of 100 million greeting cards Toyota is sending out to the American public this Christmas season.

Greer, moments after announcing that the 2008 Corolla would be the official car of sitting down with loved ones and reminiscing about years past. "We got trapped in a bidding war with General Motors over the sound of carolers beneath an open window, but it was worth it in the end."

"After all, yuletide spirit is everywhere you look," Greer added. "Or, I should say, 'Toyota Presents: Yuletide Spirit' is everywhere you look."

Toyota's marketing campaign has reportedly increased sales figures by 3 percent in the last week alone, and investors are hopeful that the deal will continue to spread the holiday message of generosity, compassion for others, superior handling on all luxury 4Runners, good tidings, antilock brakes on every SUV and year-end truck, and faith in your fellow man.

"We've enjoyed a steady increase in revenue since becoming a proud supporter of warming up with a hot cup of cocoa," Toyota promotions director Kyle Williamson said. "Plus, sponsoring that priceless smile on your wife's face Christmas morning will only open more potential growth markets to us."

Toyota is not the first company to make a cross-promotional deal with a popular indefinable entity, however. In 2002, Johnson & Johnson secured a partnership with a mother's unconditional love for her child, while Budweiser paired up with a teenager's desire to escape feelings of social anxiety and confusion in 2005.

Despite Toyota's initial success, many market analysts claim that the car company may have overpaid for its abstract product placement.

"This might have been a smart move in the 1950s, or even the '60s, when holiday cheer was still alive and well," *Car & Driver* reporter and family black sheep Malcolm Jones said. "But these days, Toyota could have gotten twice the exposure for half the cost had it sponsored holiday depression and ill will instead. And if they had been willing to buy out Lean Cuisine frozen meals' stake in post–New Year's resignation and apathy, the ad tie-ins could have extended well into January."

"'After all, yuletide spirit is everywhere you look. Or, should I say, 'Toyota Presents: Yuletide Spirit' is everywhere you look.'"

While only time will tell what effect the marketing subterfuge will ultimately have on consumers, Toyota's tactics have already angered a number of Americans.

"The holidays shouldn't be about consumerism—they should be about faith, and hope, and the simple pleasures in life," Chicago resident Samantha Bryant said. "Like the all-new Toyota Camry, for instance." 🖉

Only Positive Statistic Of Year Announced

WASHINGTON—Amid a growing list of domestic and international concerns such as skyrocketing fuel prices, the slumping dollar, massive recalls of tainted food, the housing market collapse, and an increase in obesity, the American Society for the Prevention of Cruelty to Animals delivered the country's only positive statistic Tuesday when officials announced that cases of feline leukemia had stabilized. "In this current climate, we were all waiting for some good news," said Brad Gambrell, 37, an unemployed census worker. "With more infants perishing during childbirth, fewer citizens covered by health insurance, and air quality steadily worsening, it's a huge relief that the number of cats dying from this horrible disease is staying the same." Additional data showed that, upon hearing the news, hundreds of Americans who were being evicted from their homes or learning that they had colon cancer briefly experienced a glimmer of hope—a once-common sensation that has declined by 250 percent since 2002.

Christmas Brought To Iraq By Force

BAGHDAD, IRAQ—On almost every corner in Iraq's capital city, carolers are singing, trees are being trimmed, and shoppers are rushing home with their packages—all under the watchful eye of U.S. troops dedicated to bringing the magic of Christmas to Iraq by force.

"It's important that life in liberated Iraq get back to normal as soon as possible," said Deputy Defense Secretary Paul Wolfowitz at a press conference Monday. "That's why we're making sure that Iraqis have the best Christmas ever—something they certainly wouldn't have had under Saddam Hussein's regime."

To that end, 25,000 troops from the 3rd Armored Cavalry Regiment and 82nd Airborne Division have been deployed. Their missions include the distribution of cookies and eggnog at major Iraqi city centers, the conscription of bell-ringers from among the Iraqi citizenry, and the enforcement of a new policy in which every man, woman, and child in Baghdad pays at least one visit to 'Twas The Night...On Ice.

Immediately following the press conference, high-altitude bombers began to string Christmas lights throughout the greater-Baghdad area, and Wild Weasel electronic-warfare fighter jets initiated 24-hour air patrols to broadcast Bing Crosby's "White Christmas" over the nation. Armored columns struck out from all major allied firebases to erect a Christmas tree in the town square of every city, while foot soldiers placed fully lit, heavily guarded nativity scenes in front of every Iraqi mosque.

"Thus far, Operation Desert Santa has gone off without a hitch," said Gen. Stanley Kimmet, commander of U.S. armed

U.S. soldiers instruct an Iraqi to tell Santa what he wants for Christmas.

CHRISTMAS EXPOSED

reconnaissance-and-mistletoe operations in the volatile Tikrit region of central Iraq. "There has been sporadic house-to-house fighting during our door-to-door caroling, but that's to be expected in a Christmas season of this magnitude."

According to Lt. Gen. Ricardo Sanchez, the top American military commander in Iraq, every precaution is being taken to ensure the peaceful enforcement of the Christmas season in occupied Iraq.

"All American military personnel have been instructed that the observation of Christmas should be carried out efficiently and tastefully, with minimal emphasis on the season's commercial aspects," said Sanchez, who addressed reporters while a decorations division strung wreaths and garlands outside his headquarters. "We must keep in mind that the reason for the season-oriented campaign is for Iraq to celebrate the birth of our Lord and Savior Jesus Christ."

An aide for Sanchez later explained that, in order to ensure a meaningful holiday season for all Iraqis, provisions were made for those Iraqis who elected to observe Hanukkah.

A mosque in Baghdad decorated by U.S. troops.

Like many U.S. operations in Iraq, Operation Desert Santa has met with some resistance. A convoy transporting fruitcake and gingerbread came under rocket attack Sunday night just outside Checkpoint Noël in Basra, and unidentified bands of Iraqis exchanged gunfire with Marines operating an armored Humvee simulated sleigh ride in a Baghdad suburb. In spite of these troubles, regional commanders report progress, with only eight U.S. casualties resulting from the operation.

Still, Iraqis report that they are unable to get into the Christmas spirit.

"Why am I supposed to feel joy for the world?" said 34-year-old Baghdad mechanic Hassan al-Ajili as he stood in line for his mandatory visit with Santa. "My country is still at

---

"'Now, for some reason, men with machine guns have placed two rows of jingling antlered pigs on the roof of our house.'"

---

war. I need an American identification card to get anywhere in my own city. Now, for some reason, men with machine guns have placed two rows of jingling antlered pigs on the roof of our house. This is insane."

Bush, speaking from his Crawford ranch, praised the brave men and women of Operation Desert Santa and asked for the understanding of all Americans.

"We must be patient with the Iraqis," said Bush, seated before a Christmas tree dotted with Scottish terrier ornaments. "The holidays can be a very stressful time, especially for people not yet used to the customs. I'm sure Iraq will enjoy the happiest of holiday seasons if we show resolve and commit to making sure that they do."

President Bush then called for 30,000 new troops to be deployed in the next week to ensure an effective and precise enforcement of Christmas throughout the region. Salvation and 8th Army detachments will be stationed on every corner by Christmas Eve to make sure that every last Iraqi citizen spends the holiday at home, with family.

Sanchez said he is confident that he can meet that deadline.

"A merry Christmas in Iraq means peace in the Middle East has finally been achieved," Sanchez said. "God bless us, every one." 𝄞

Recalled Holiday Toys

The U.S. Consumer Product Safety Commission recently released its annual list of recalled toys. Which items should parents avoid buying?

▶ "I'm An Eye Surgeon!" Play Kit

▶ Li'l Professor Kinsey's Sexual Chemistry Set

▶ SpongeBob CrazyPants Electric Spaz-Out Doll With Medication

▶ "Scaredy Mommy" Brand Totally Non-Toxic, Rounded-Edge Plastic Play Slab

▶ My First Sock With A Brick In it

▶ Baby Strobey Nightlight

▶ Uncle Harry's Uncannily Well-Done Fun Money

▶ Black Widow Barbie With Mate 'N' Kill Action

▶ Crap-In-The-Pants Family Fun Game

▶ Harvey Keitel's Pre-School Of Hard Knocks Learning Set

Real-Life Grinch Celebrates 'Hanukkah'

FREDONIA, KS—A real-life Grinch was found Monday in Fredonia, where, unlike his fellow residents, Josh Baum refuses to celebrate Christmas. "I'm looking forward to a nice Hanukkah," the Yuletide-shunning misanthrope said. "We'll be lighting the same menorah that's been in my family for generations." Baum would not comment on the possibility that spontaneous Christmas caroling would cause his small heart to grow three sizes.

The Pagan Deviltry Of The Christ's Mass Holiday And How We Must Resist Its Temptation

By Reverend Angus Hustings

The Winter Solstice has not yet fallen upon us, yet the Parish is already cover'd in a dense Blanket of Snow; the Boys of our Town Ship, I am sorry to testify, have cast aside their School Primers and Lunch Encasements to build Ramparts of Snow, and to heave Spheres of a kindr'd Nature at one another in great Jollity and lightness of Spirit.

I discover'd this whilst arduously negotiating my Way across the Publick Square, during which it was my abject Misfortune to be struck by one of these Snow Projectiles; its Velocity drove the Stove Pipe Hat from my Head.

I was quite Scarlet with Rage, and I swiftly box'd the Ears of the churlish young Hobbledehoy who lobb'd the offending Missile. For the Hat was a cherish'd Gift from an esteem'd Prelate of our Synod who was a Class Mate of mine at Seminary so many Years ago. The purblind Urchin could only whimper in Reply and alleg'd that it was merely unintentional Happenstance. But I knew my Cause was just; for did not David the King spake unto the Lord, "Thou hast also given me the Necks of mine Enemies, that I might destroy them that hate me"?

I promptly seiz'd the Whelp by his smarting Ear and led him to his Master, whom I knew as the Town Green Grocer. The Green Grocer thank'd me for my Attentions, claiming that he was sorely behind in his Labours, and need'd his Boy to affix Price Labels onto a great Multitude of Fruit Roll Ups.

The Boy set to loud Moaning, and sobb'd that he was most weary of engaging in this particular Trade, as he was fast losing the Sensation in his Wrists; but the Green Grocer gave him a great Clout and told him to mind. The Grocer then explain'd unto me that, being as it is the joyous Season of the Christ's Mass, the Boy's Mind fairly dances with Visions of Sugar Plums and other rare Yule Tide Delights, and he is less apt to apply himself to more sobering Tasks.

Verily, I would not have been more shock'd and appall'd if he had said that The Boy was the Devil himself. For the Holiday known as the Christ's Mass is fraught with Pagan Deviltry that finds no Liturgical Justification in the Holy Scriptures.

Where in the Gospels does it mention that, to honor the Birth of our Divine Saviour, one must adorn an Ever Green Tree with gild'd Spangles and Baubles? Or that gaily disguis'd Sundries be plac'd under this Tree, to be exchang'd later as Idolatrous Tokens of Good Will amongst Lov'd Ones? Or that one may, with one's Bosom Companions, regale the Homes of one's Town Ship with melodious Carols, imbibe the Nog compris'd of Eggs, feast upon the Hart, cut merry Capers, await the Coming of a beard'd Gentle Man upon a Sledge drawn by Elk, and glide upon the frozen Pond in Blad'd Shoes? Not a Trace of this is to be found in the Good Book.

I submit that such Expressions of Holiday Cheer are of the purest Heresy; and did not our Divine Saviour say unto the Scribes and Pharisees, "He that shall blaspheme against the Holy Ghost hath never Forgiveness, but is in Danger of eternal Damnation"? The truly Pious will observe the Christ's Mass Tide as they would any other Day of the Year: swath'd in a Hair Shirt and scourging oneself repeatedly with a Cow Hide.

When I first became Rector of this Parish, I was most shock'd and vex'd to find that my Predecessor had institut'd a yearly Pageant to commemorate the Christ's Mass Holiday. In this Pageant, a Number of Children were adorn'd to resemble the Holy Family, the Magi, Shepherds, and Angels. After they perform'd the Story of the Nativity, the Congregation gather'd around a gaudily bedeck'd Yule Tree and ate Johnny Cakes bak'd to resemble Stars and Bells.

"Where in the Gospels does it mention that, to honor the Birth of our Divine Saviour, one must adorn an Ever Green Tree with gild'd Spangles and Baubles? Or That gaily disguis'd Sundries be plac'd under this Tree, to be exchang'd later as Idolatrous Tokens of Good Will amongst Lov'd Ones?"

Then, the Pastor, dress'd as the beard'd Father of Christ's Mass, pass'd out Gifts to the Young. I would have none of that. Instead of permitting the Children to masquerade immodestly as Angels and Saints, I lock'd them in my Rectory Study, and drill'd them endlessly in the rote Memorization of the Book of Numbers.

Alas, the Temptation to indulge in the barbarous Festivities of the Christ's Mass is great indeed, as I bore Witness in the very Parsonage in which I, the Good Woman Hustings and our eight Off Spring dwell. One Evening before the Day of the Christ's Mass, as I was about to douse the Parlor Hearth, I heard a faint Creaking upon the Ceiling. I determin'd that the Noise was emanating from the Sleeping Quarters of my Children. Furious that they had disobeyed their strict Bed Time of Seven O'Clock, I swiftly made my way Up Stairs and flung open the Door of their Chamber. I was absolutely Aghast to find them huddled upon the Floor, preparing to divide into Portions a small Plum Pudding.

My Wrath waxing most Hot, I seiz'd my eldest Son, Neville, by his coarse Sack Cloth Garment, and gave him a sound Shake, for I consider'd him responsible for leading his younger siblings Astray. "What?" I cried unto them. "Have you forsaken all that you have been taught in the Bible of the Lord our God and chosen to adopt the Ways of the Ungodly, as did the Children of Israel when they shunn'd the Covenant of God and worshiped the Molten Calf?"

"If you please, Sir," Neville simpered. "The Pudding was a Gift of a Neighbor Lady, who took Pity upon us, that we had no Christ's Mass Cheer of our own. She cook'd it upon her very Hearth herself, and present'd it to us when you were away, so that we may enjoy the Good Tidings of the Blessed Season."

Great was my Anguish, as I realiz'd that my Years of Tireless Preaching had borne rotten Fruit. As Punishment, I forc'd my Children to sleep upon Nettles, drink rancid Gravy. and recite the Book of Leviticus before they could go to the Out House.

For did not Moses speak unto all Israel, "The Lord shall establish thee an holy People unto Himself, as He hath sworn unto thee, if thou shalt keep the Commandments of the Lord thy God, and walk in his Ways"? And none of his Ways include the Eating of the Plum Pudding, and the Viewing of the Elk with the Crimson Nose upon the Television Set. With that in Mind, may Peace be unto you, in the Name of the Father, and the Son, and the Holy Ghost, Amen. ∅

Area Stores Stock Up On Shit

CHICAGO—With the official start of the holiday season just days away, Chicago retailers—like those across the U.S.—are bracing for the coming onslaught of shoppers with an unprecedented stockup on shit.

In anticipation of the hordes of shoppers the holiday season brings, area retailers are busy filling their shelves with shit.

"You wouldn't believe how much shit we are selling," said Amos Frawley, manager of a Chicago-area Wal-Mart store. "Electric razors, *Toy Story* videos, novelty ties, football phones, Hickory Farms cheese-and-meat gift sets—you name it, they're buying it. We're packing every inch of shelf space with shit, and we still can't keep up with the demand."

Among the shit expected to reach new sales levels this year is Christmas-themed shit, such as shiny tree decorations and ceramic, hand-painted Santa figurines. Also expected to sell well are articles of clothing which light up at night, such as glow-in-the-dark Joe Boxer–brand boxer shorts and battery-operated Dearfoam slippers with special "Nite-Lites" attached to the front.

"Novelty shit always seems to sell well," said Elaine Maier, head apparel buyer for an area Marshall Field's department store. "Then again, around this time of year, people will buy just about any shit they can get their hands on."

Woodfield Mall in Schaumburg, IL, is getting into the spirit of the holidays—and of selling loads of shit—by decorating its courtyard in a "Wonderland of Shit" motif featuring Christmas-themed shit from all 172 of its stores. Actor Jeff Goldblum is slated to appear at the mall Friday to officially kick off the festivities by reciting his famous *Jurassic Park* line, "That is one big pile of shit."

> "Toys "R" Us, the nation's largest toy retailer, is aggressively promoting its seasonal slogan, 'The shit you want at the best prices.'"

Though Christmas is still weeks away, the shopping has already hit a fever pitch. "I got to the mall at 6 a.m. today, two hours before it even opened," said Edgar Janks of DeKalb, IL. "I want first crack at the shit. Nobody wants to get there after all the good shit's gone."

Said Chicago's Debra Tanner, who was at the mall Monday to buy a large amount of shit, including a cordless phone, a Charlotte Hornets NBA Starter jacket, and a five-speed foot massager: "I don't have nearly enough time to get the shit I need."

Lower prices are also expected to spur purchases of shit this year. Toys "R" Us, the nation's largest toy retailer, is aggressively promoting its seasonal slogan, "The shit you want at the best prices."

"Not only is there more shit this year than ever before," said noted economist Milton Friedenzohn, "but what there is is far shittier. The Sanyo boom boxes being sold this year, for example, are even more likely to break than those from the previous year. And those new Panasonic WebTVs are just shit."

In addition to familiar retailers, shops specializing in seasonal shit are opening temporarily in hopes of capitalizing on the December craving for shit. "Christmas Shit," "Wicks 'n' Shit," and "Bob's Shittery" are just a few of the stores offering customers nothing but shit.

Even supermarkets are altering their inventories to meet the demand for shit, filling shelves with decorative snack tins featuring depictions of Santa Claus, which cost twice as much as comparable items that come in ordinary packaging. Also available are pfefferneuse cookies, eggnog, and holiday Oreo cookies with red shit inside.

> "In addition to familiar retailers, shops specializing in seasonal shit are opening temporarily in hopes of capitalizing on the December craving for shit. 'Christmas Shit,' 'Wicks 'n' Shit,' and 'Bob's Shittery' are just a few of the stores offering customers nothing but shit."

Said Friedenzohn: "There's going be a whole lot of shit under America's Christmas trees this year." ⌀

Top Corporate Holiday Gifts

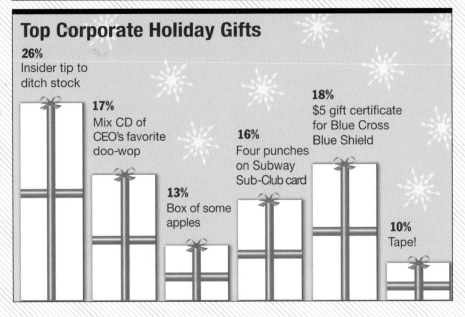

26%
Insider tip to
ditch stock

17%
Mix CD of
CEO's favorite
doo-wop

13%
Box of some
apples

16%
Four punches
on Subway
Sub-Club card

18%
$5 gift certificate
for Blue Cross
Blue Shield

10%
Tape!

44 Suspicious Packages Detonated Under White House Christmas Tree

Holiday Advertisers Seek Coveted Dicktard Demographic

NEW YORK—The advertising blitz before the holiday shopping season seems to come earlier and earlier, and this year is no exception, with more retailers than ever seeking to tap into the seemingly limitless spending power of the highly desirable dicktard demographic.

"Since Thanksgiving, the advertising industry has spent over $1 billion to influence what American dicktards, asswipes, and cock-knobs will put under their Christmas trees," Merrill Lynch retail analyst Barbour Scott said. "By the third week in December, that number is expected to quadruple, as the courting process intensifies for the gnat-like attention of these witless lamebrains."

Dicktard spending dollars, as well as those of the smaller but ever more important dickweed and dipstick market segments, can mean the difference between a fourth-quarter boom or bust for major retailers.

"The major chains can no longer just stock their shelves and expect the dicktards to come pouring in," Scott said. "They need to be told where to go and what to buy—10 million NASCAR toilet seats don't sell themselves."

The dicktard demographic—a nationwide consumer base that crosses all economic classes and levels of income—was once the sole province of dullard-friendly superstores like Wal-Mart and Sears. But in recent years, these companies have lost

Dicktards flock to major shopping centers this season.

market share to smaller outlets and online stores, which allow not only dicktards, but asshats and douchelords as well, to consume more products faster.

"The competition for the dicktard spender is unbelievably fierce," said Scott, who also follows trends among cuntlicks and fuckbrains. "Retailers target shoppers who will buy a $5 item for $50, or who will purchase an electric card-shuffler on a whim, only to lose interest in it two weeks later, clearing the way for even more impulse buying the following quarter."

Within the dicktard segment are a series of specific subsets, including bitch-holes, known for their fleeting emotional attachment to products such as scented candles and baby figurines, and shitwads, who often spend up to 45 percent of their annual income on expensive electronics and pricey upgrades to expensive electronics.

"Within the dicktard segment are a series of specific subsets, including bitch-holes and shitwads."

and Abercrombie & Fitch were among the most successful at luring buyers to their checkout aisles. Target has shown early promise this year by marketing directly to dicktards with the brightly colored and inoffensive ad campaign "Holiday Magic—You Deserve It."

"We truly don't care what kind of crap these people buy, as long as it's our crap," Target CEO Bob Ulrich said. "Throw in some flattery, make them think that the decision to come to our store was made out of their own free will—that seems to work. Whatever it takes to get these lard-ass nimrods into our stores, we're going to do it."

As the holiday shopping season takes off, manufacturers are also reaching out to dicktards with ads appealing to their inherent attraction to lifestyles that do not, in actuality, approximate their own.

"Who, outside of professional carpenters and maybe a few serious woodworking hobbyists, honestly needs a HandiSaw?" said Black & Decker spokesman Rory Cantwell, referring to the cordless tool his company has marketed to fuckfaced noobs as a holiday gift favorite. "These puds have no use for it and, in fact, could seriously injure themselves with it. But if we just pitch it as this handy way for real men to cut through stuff, they go flying off the shelves. Same goes for our Power Mop, which, again, is completely useless."

"Dicktard spending dollars, as well as those of the smaller but ever more important dickweed and dipstick market segments, can mean the difference between a fourth-quarter boom or bust for major retailers."

While no retail chain could decisively claim the dicktard sales trophy last December, stores such as Target, Best Buy,

"And if we can work a pair of boobs and an American flag into the ads, we're virtually guaranteed holiday green," he added. ∅

Pony-Wanting Ron Artest To Be On Best Behavior Till Christmas

INDIANAPOLIS—Just over one year since Ron Artest climbed into the stands at the Palace of Auburn Hills and took a swing at a fan, resulting in a suspension, a fine, and an empty stocking, the Pacers forward said that he has learned from his mistakes, and knows that any misstep on or off the court during the 2005 holiday season could severely hurt his chances of getting that pony he's been asking for. "Last year, I let my emotions get the best of me—I let down my teammates, my fans, my family, myself, and Santa," Artest said. "Now that I know I'm being watched and scrutinized, I'm going to make an extra-special effort to be nice, whether it means keeping my temper in check during an in-game flare-up, or helping do chores around the house. It's the only way to earn back the respect I need to get Princess." Artest added that after Christmas, any critics, opponents, or fans "better be on their best behavior," as he is making a New Year's resolution to punch someone.

How Very Special

I don't have to tell you Jeanketeers that Christmas is just around the corner, which means it's time for—you got it—TV Christmas specials. Even though I eagerly welcome the return of trusty old Rudolph and Frosty (who doesn't?), there's one type of special that's missing these days, and that's the old variety-show type with real singers and dancers. You know, like Andy Williams and Perry Como. Maybe some of you old-timers out there (don't worry, I won't give away your ages!!) remember the days when big music stars weren't too "cool" to wear red sweaters, drink steaming hot chocolate, and welcome a children's choir into their ski lodge.

A Room Of Jean's Own
By Jean Teasdale

What if one of the networks gave your old pal Jean a pile of money and let her direct her own holiday special? Well, it would go a little something like this...

Over a beautiful country snow scene, fade in. The title credits: "Jean Teasdale's Ho-Ho-Ho-larious Christmas! Sponsored by Reunite, Dolley Madison, Norelco, and Hallmark Cards." (Just like the old specials!) Then two dozen dancers in dazzling silver and gold costumes trimmed with white fur rush into view, spinning and frolicking. Only, unlike typical holiday-special dancers, they aren't skinny and leggy—they're all different sizes and shapes. Well, mostly sort of plump, like me. But no one tells them they aren't good enough or sexy enough. This special is all about inclusion.

Then the dancers line up in front of a charming, life-size gingerbread house and say in unison, "Ladies and gentlemen, here she is, that real-life vision of sugarplums herself, Jean Teasdale!" (Or something like that.) And then I come out, dressed in a long green skirt that looks like a conifer tree, and I sing "Rockin' Around The Christmas Tree." (Technically, I don't sing very well, but this special would be all about fun and not judging, as well as inclusion.) And of course, everyone dances around me, and at the end of the song, there's a flash, and it's revealed that the dancers have transformed into tiny ornaments and cover my skirt! Imaginative, huh?

Now, every Christmas special has its little storyline. Here's mine: It's Christmas Eve, and I've sent hubby Rick to the store for Tom & Jerry mix, but soon afterwards, it started to snow, and he hasn't been seen or heard from for hours.

> "And then I come out, dressed in a long green skirt that looks like a conifer tree, and I sing 'Rockin' Around The Christmas Tree.' (Technically, I don't sing very well, but this special would be all about fun and not judging, as well as inclusion.)"

But of course, it's a holiday special, so there's plenty of comedy, music, and cheer to offset the gloom. Guest number one is none other than my crazy pal Fulgencio, the jolliest elf you've ever seen! "Girl, you look fabu!" he says in his boisterous way. (I'm no longer wearing the Christmas tree skirt, but a more comfortable and beautifully sequined sweatsuit.) I say I'm worried about Rick, and Fulgencio tells me that it's just as well he's not around, because get a load of what he has for me. In rolls a huge present. Fulgencio unties the bow, and out pops—be still, my heart—Patrick Swayze! "You've always been my biggest fan, Jean, and in the spirit of giving, this is for you," he says, tenderly taking my hand in his. He sings me the hottest version of "Merry Christmas Baby" ever, 10 times better than Elvis. It's all I can do to keep from bawling! Then, as a further surprise, Patrick Swayze suddenly turns into a gigantic chocolate statue, and Fulgencio and I eat him! (Nutty, huh?)

"'Girl, you look fabu!' he says in his boisterous way. (I'm no longer wearing the Christmas tree skirt, but a more comfortable and beautiful sequined sweatsuit.)"

I haven't quite worked out the middle yet. I'm not sure if I should make Christmas cookies with Rosie O'Donnell (dressed as a nutcracker) or have an ice-skating segment inspired by *Ice Castles*. I'll definitely have a performance by the reunited ABBA, and also a segment of formal apologies from all the people who've fired me throughout the years. In the spirit of the season, I will forgive them all and invite them in to warm themselves at my hearth.

Bam! Bam! Who's that at my door? Why, it's none other than the Queen Diva herself, Miss Piggy! Miss Piggy is mad at me because she thinks she deserves to have her own special. To remind her about the

Christmas spirit (and to keep from getting karate-chopped!), I coax her into singing "We Need A Little Christmas" with a bunch of adorable children dressed as Tiny Tim.

It's Christmas Eve and nearing midnight, and still no sign of Rick. I'm getting really worried. I don my fur-trimmed bonnet and cloak and set out to look for him. The land is beautiful and moonlit but sort of eerie at the same time. I approach a clearing and look up, and see a huge, looming figure in front of me! Oh, no—could it be the Abominable Snowman?

After the commercial break, I'm still cowering before the looming giant. But suddenly I realize that it's only a shadow being cast by hubby Rick! Jugs of Tom & Jerry mix in tow, he explains that he got lost in the snowstorm on his way back from the store. "But then I saw a very bright star shining in the heavens," he explains. "It cast a light down a path, and I followed the path, and a little while later, our house was in view." We sing "Silent Night," which is religious without being preachy.

No sooner do we get inside than we hear sleigh bells on the roof! Some loose soot and masonry tumbles into the fireplace. It's Santa Claus! Only this isn't just any Santa Claus—it's my dad! "Merry Christmas, Jeannie my daughter!" he cries. Everybody gasps in wonder, but I just groan. "He's actually a phony shopping-mall Santa," I say. "He left town earlier this year when his business failed, and he never paid me for all the work I did for him." But that's where I'm wrong—Dad reveals that he *really* is Santa. His eyes twinkle, he puts his finger to his red nose, and suddenly a huge pile of money and presents, all for me, materializes under my tree! Everybody cheers, and we all sing "Santa Claus Is Coming To Town."

After the final commercial break, I come out on the now-darkened set carrying a candle. I thank everybody for watching my special, and reading my column for all these years. I say that you're my favorite guest stars of all, and if I had one wish, it would be that everybody could have a holiday just like a holiday special. Oh, and also, I say that I'm looking for a job again, and if you know anyone who's hiring, let me know. 🌿

Drinking Responsibly During The Holidays

The holiday season is a time to enjoy family dinners, office parties, and get-togethers with friends. Festive drinks and tasty punches often contribute to the holiday revelry, so here are some tips to help you celebrate sensibly:

- If you are a woman, remember: Women are more sensitive to the effects of alcohol. If you are a man, remember: Women are more sensitive to the effects of alcohol.

- Always drink from the bottle labeled "XXX." The bottle with the skull-and-crossbones on the front is poison.

- Drinking alone is a telltale sign that you know better than to put up with anybody's bullshit.

- Drinking more than seven nights a week is not just irresponsible, it's impossible.

- If someone you know is too drunk to drive, demand that he let you have his car keys. If he refuses, pull out a gun and demand the car keys again. This also works with people who are not drunk, and whom you do not know.

- Never drink with Tyler Schneeklov.

- While standing in the middle of the road at 3 a.m. yelling expletives at your ex-girlfriend, wear light-colored clothing so motorists can see you.

- Once you get married and have kids, stop drinking tons of whiskey and switch to drinking tons of wine.

- Always re-cap your flask between swigs. This lengthens the amount of time between drinks.

- Don't mix alcohol with stereotypes. If you are Irish, drink rum. If you are a pirate, drink whiskey.

- Don't drink and drive. Disregard this tip if you happen to be one of those people who drive better drunk.

- If you suddenly find yourself impaired by alcohol, prevent any social awkwardness by informing all those present that you profoundly love them, and that you never get this drunk.

- Never use alcohol to escape feelings of failure and loneliness. Use Vicodin.

- Before heading out to the office holiday party, tape a handcuff key to the inside of your watchband. Just trust us on this one.

Area Man Can Actually Feel The Advanced Vapor Action Working

ELMIRA, NY—Local resident Maurice Weathers enjoyed temporary relief from congestion and minor throat irritation Monday thanks to the fast-acting advanced vapor action of Halls Mentho-lyptus™ cough drops.

Maurice Weathers (inset) breathes in the wavy, sinus-clearing vapors of doctor-recommended Halls Mentho-lyptus cough drops.

"It's a proven fact that Halls, the brand you've trusted for nearly a century, alleviates the discomfort associated with cold-related coughs for as much as 12 hours," said Dr. Richard Marin, an ears, nose, and throat specialist at the famed Mayo Clinic in Rochester, MN. "But don't take my word for it: Take Maurice Weathers'."

"When I first heard about Halls, I was skeptical," said Weathers, who had been suffering from flu symptoms since Dec. 3. "Other leading cough-drop brands had failed me before. And this was one tough cold."

Weathers said his wife Nicole urged him to try the product, saying that her grandmother "used to swear by it." "When Nicole said that, I thought to myself, 'Her grandmother? That must have been an aw-ful long time ago,'" Weathers said. "Times have changed, and so have colds."

Despite his reservations, after more urging from his wife, Weathers took a Halls.

> ## "'When Nicole said that, I thought to myself, 'Her grandmother? That must have been an awful long time ago,' Weathers said. 'Times have changed, and so have colds.'"

"I figured, what could it hurt? I'll give it a shot," Weathers said. "And you know what? Just one lozenge cleared my nasal passages and soothed the redness in my throat within minutes. I could actually feel the advanced vapor action working."

So effective was the advanced vapor action of Halls, Weathers was back on his feet in just minutes.

"Nicole just about did a double take when she saw me wearing my overcoat and toting my briefcase as I headed for the door," Weathers said. "She said to me, 'I thought you called in sick. What's wrong?'"

Continued Weathers: "I just held up the roll of Halls she gave me and said with a smile, 'You mean, what's right?!'"

> **"'Nicole just about did a double take when she saw me wearing my overcoat and toting my briefcase as I headed for the door. She said to me, "I thought you called in sick. What's wrong?" I just held up the roll of Halls she gave me and said with a smile, 'You mean, what's right?!'"**

Halls spokesman Howard Rubenstein said he is not surprised by Weathers' success with the product.

"With cold and flu season upon us, people want relief—fast," Rubenstein said. "And the advanced vapor action of Halls provides just that. Containing "mentho-lyptus," an active ingredient distilled from eucalyptus leaves, Halls is laboratory-proven to relieve the throat soreness associated with coughs and colds."

"And now, with new Aspen Wintermint and Soothing Strawberry flavors," Rubenstein said, "advanced vapor action never tasted so good."

Added Rubenstein: "If Dr. Josiah Halls, the young Columbia University chemistry student who first synthesized mentho-lyptus and blended it into glucose lozenges in 1924, could see what his invention has done for cold and flu sufferers the world over, he would be proud."

One of those sufferers—or, rather, former sufferers—won't ever doubt the power of Halls again.

"Advanced vapor action—who would have known it could be so effective?" Weathers asked. "But just one Halls gave me relief for hours. So long, other leading brands. From now on, it's Halls for me." ⌀

Stocking Up For Weather Emergencies

In anticipation of the snowstorms that paralyzed the Mid-Atlantic, store shelves were stripped bare, leaving some unlucky citizens without the bare essentials. Here are the items you should not be without if you're snowed in:

- **Jigsaw puzzles:** If you can't get out of the house, an old-fashioned jigsaw puzzle is the perfect way to while away the hours, and the perfect catalyst for a fight with your family or roommates when you get sick of doing the same puzzle for four hours

- **Lean Cuisine Swedish meatballs:** Suddenly this doesn't look quite so bad anymore, eh, Snow Prisoner?

- **Digital camera:** Immediately after the storm, you'll need to take pictures of the mounds of snow outside, upload them to Facebook, and enter such captions as "enough snow for you?" or "MY CAR IS UNDER THERE SOMEWHERE LOL!!!!!"

- **Pfeifer Zeliska .600 Nitro Express revolver:** This powerful handgun will stop any… wild game…you are hunting in order to keep your family fed and warm (wink wink)

- **Headlamp flashlight:** So the rescue team can find you and carry out your corpse

- **Five gallons of bleach:** As long as you're stuck inside you might as well get some cleaning done

- **Gender-specific sex toy:** Heavy snow accumulation will make roads impassible, and your weekly visit to a prostitute unlikely

- **Tauntaun:** When your best friend goes missing in the blizzard conditions, you'll need to use the carcass of this bipedal reptomammal to keep his body warm

Why Can't We Have A Nice Igloo Like The Meekitjuks Next Door?

By Komangapik Mukpa

This so-called "igloo" of ours, dear, is a complete embarrassment. Some days, I don't even want to be seen crawling out of the entrance. Now, the Meekitjuks next door, they've got a beautiful place— perfectly cut blocks of ice, a nice, wide entrance, and a two-sled snow rampart built into the back. Why can't we live in a decent igloo like them?

Just take a look at this poor excuse for an igloo: there are ice shavings all over the floor, the ceiling is filthy with smoke, and the wall that faces the rising sun is so uneven, it looks like it's ready to cave in at any second. I wouldn't be surprised if we came home one day to find the whole dome collapsed! Yes, we're the laughingstock of the whole neighborhood.

Yesterday, I had some of the gals from the neighborhood over for a bit of blood soup. I didn't even have a decent hammered-copper bowl to serve it in. On top of that, do you think they didn't notice the worn-out condition of our qipiik? It's more hole than caribou hide! And this old polar-bear-skin rug—it's an ancient hand-me-down from my grandmother, and we're still using it.

All the other women in the village enjoy the latest modern conveniences: blades made of metal, coffee cans to cure the blubber dip. Meanwhile, I don't have so much as an *ulu* knife to butcher the darn seals.

Not that I've had much to butcher lately. Yesterday, I was peeking out the front entrance and saw Pauloosie Meekitjuk come home after a day of hunting. He was dragging two seals home on his sled! When was the last time you brought two seals home? Last week, it was a few skinny little otters. You're always giving the same lame excuse, telling me it's a "hard winter." Well, we must have some real strange weather patterns around these parts, because it doesn't seem to be a hard winter 20 feet away over at Chez Meekitjuk.

You come home every night, complaining about how exhausted you are from standing over the ice all day with a harpoon, waiting for a seal to surface. And that's not even counting all the nights you come crawling in the front hole at 2 a.m., armed with some phony-baloney story

> "He was dragging two seals home on his sled! When was the last time you brought two seals home? Last week, it was a few skinny little otters."

about how you've been out all night following caribou tracks across the frozen tundra. Please. I'm not stupid. I know you're down at the kashgee listening to the shaman stories with the guys. And you know what? I'm really starting to get tired of it.

This coming Sunday, we're invited to the seal-sharing feast over at the Meekitjuks. You'll be happy to know that there will be a whole feast of sliced flipper and blubber and caribou-stomach contents. And I'm sure you'll enjoy it every bit as much as the Meekitjuks' last feast. But we're not going to be invited too many more times if you don't bring home a seal soon to return the favor. Then where will we be? We'll be shunned and have to move our igloo to the bad part of the village, out where the anthropologists live.

I know what you're thinking: "But Komangapik! We just got a new kayak this year! Doesn't that count for something?" Some kayak! The Meekitjuks have a 14-foot kayak, and ours is barely 10 feet long. And what about the caribou-skin interior you keep saying you'll put in it as soon as you get the time? You promised to do it 20 moons ago!

> ## "Please. I'm not stupid. I know you're down at the kashgee listening to the shaman stories with the guys. And you know what? I'm really starting to get tired of it."

The only thing you care about is that stupid sled of yours. Did we really need another dog? I think Qallunaaq and Kitikmeot were more than adequate, but you insisted we needed Nujuattaittut and Nujuattaittuttuta, too.

My mother warned me about you. She said, "Komangapik, that man has the spirit of the mighty humpback whale in his soul, but nothing but dust in the pockets of his parka." What did I know? I was only 14. Now that I'm older, I understand all too well what she was saying.

Don't I deserve a decent igloo? Do you think I just sit around all day chewing dried salmon while you're away hunting? Yesterday, I spent all day repairing last year's sealskin boots with sinew thread and bone needles, just so I'd have something decent to wear to storytelling sessions around the group fire. If only I could have something besides the same old fox-fur coats.

You spare no expense when it comes to your precious harpoons and knives. You just had to have that toggle harpoon made out of ivory when the antler one would have done fine. But as soon as I want a few small things for around the igloo, we suddenly don't have the skins to trade for them.

Did you see the wooden mask Amik Meekitjuk has on her wall? I asked her where she got it. She said she bought it during an umiak trip to Baffin Island and that it cost *only* a pot of seal oil. Only! We barely have enough seal oil to keep our igloo lit through the winter, and they're trading away a whole pot of oil! The fact that she got it during a trip to Baffin Island only makes it worse. Every year, you promise that the whole family will migrate there for the summer to fish and capture birds. Then, when it's time to go, you take off with the other men and say there's not enough room in the umiak for me and the kids.

Do you think I enjoy sitting home, staring at the same one wall day after day? Of course not! Then, when I offer to accompany you on the hunt, you say I talk too much and prevent the seals from coming to the surface! Well, maybe if I had more otter to skin, I'd have less time to talk. Hmmph. ∅

Study Finds Link Between Red Wine, Letting Mother Know What You Really Think

CHICAGO—Health experts have long known that drinking red wine can have such positive benefits as reducing blood vessel damage, lowering the risk of heart attack, and preventing harmful LDL cholesterol from forming. But researchers at the Northwestern University Department of Preventive Medicine have recently found that the consumption of four to six glasses of red wine, most notably at dinner or a family function, may be linked to totally going off on one's mom.

Just three glasses with dinner can support finally letting her have it.

According to a study published Monday in *The American Journal Of Medicine*, a previously unknown ingredient in red wine has been shown to cause a marked improvement of vocal clarity and emotional acuity—while reducing overall inhibition—after only four glasses.

> **"After drinking only one bottle of standard Merlot, these participants could not only remember, but could actually sing whole stretches of *Annie Get Your Gun*, even while sobbing."**

During routine trials, subjects who imbibed five glasses or more showed a remarkable increase in specific mental functions, such as the ability to recall every time their mothers had been unsupportive of their boyfriends or husbands.

A striking reduction in the time needed to translate personal epiphanies into loud, public epiphanies was also noted.

"It seems the benefits of red wine consumption are virtually limitless," said Dr. Susan Zheng, lead researcher on the study. "Many were unable to recall a single time their mother had paid more attention to their sister's soccer games than to their starring role in the school play. But after drinking only one bottle of standard Merlot, these participants could not only remember, but could actually sing whole stretches of *Annie Get Your Gun*, even while sobbing. It's extraordinary."

Dr. Zheng explained that the 100 women who participated in the study were split into two groups. One group was seated at the end of a long dinner table and subjected to backhanded compliments about their housekeeping abilities while steadily imbibing 8-ounce glasses of Turning Leaf Cabernet. The other group, a control group, was allowed to celebrate the holidays at home. ✐

NEWS IN PHOTOS

Nobody Touching Punch At CIA Christmas Party

The Times That Try Jean's Soul

Well, gang, I wish I could say that this Christmas will be the best one ever, but, judging from what's happened so far this December, I'm about ready to skip ahead to Arbor Day!

Now, before you accuse your pal Jean of taking Grinch lessons on the sly, let me assure you that I just love Christmas! If you're a shopaholic like me, it's a great excuse to exercise the old credit card! And, I gotta admit, even though I just turned 40, I still have to watch Rudolph, Frosty and all those other old Christmas specials!

A Room Of Jean's Own
By Jean Teasdale

But I also love Christmas for its true meaning, too—a time of giving and sharing stuff. And I do still believe in God and Jesus and all. (Though I haven't seen the inside of a church for almost a decade!)

Anyway, this year I decided to throw a small Christmas dinner party at my place. I hadn't entertained in years, and I felt kind of guilty about it. (About the only thing I entertain these days is the notion of going to bed early!) I also decided that this wasn't going to be a beer-and-pizza affair. No, this party would be class with a capital C! I was going to personally prepare every dish, there would be formal place settings, and the stereo would play only Andy Williams and George Winston. (With the exception of "Grandma Got Run Over By A Reindeer"— still my all-time number-one fave!)

Things started to go wrong pretty early. While I was busy basting the Rock Cornish game hens, I saw hubby Rick throwing on his jacket and heading toward the door. I asked him where he was going, and he said he was meeting up with his friend Craig over at Tacky's Tavern. (I should have known.) You can believe I put a stop to that. "I haven't been slaving in this kitchen since 9 a.m. so you could go out and get blitzed and eye the bimbos," I said. Rick whined something about having promised Craig he'd be there and said he'd only stay home if I set a place for Craig at the dinner party.

> "Craig added, 'So your wife collects dolls, eh? You need to knock her up, Rick. Or at least give her a good reaming.' You can see why I got so mad. What does collecting dolls have to do with not having children or not making whoopee?"

Well, I seriously considered saying no, because Craig, who works with Rick at the tire center, is not exactly my idea of polite company. He's the type who thinks being funny means putting someone else down. Now, heaven knows I'm pretty quick with the wisecracks myself, but I never joke in a way that makes people feel bad about things they can't help. To me, that's not humor, that's just being mean! But, in the spirit of the season, I decided to let Craig come to the party.

Well, much to my chagrin, less than 10 minutes after Rick called Tacky's, Craig came roaring in. The other guests weren't due for another hour, which meant I had to put up with Craig and Rick's loud, childish guffawing in the living room while I tossed the salad and prepared the dinner rolls in the kitchen.

Sure enough, Craig managed to get my goat right off the bat. As they sucked down Black Labels, Craig sarcastically complimented Rick on my doll collection and asked him which one he thought was the prettiest. Then Craig started teasing Rick about the fact that I keep my dolls in a tall glass curio cabinet in the living room. (Har-dee-har-har, Craig!) Rick told him to shut up, and, to further distance himself from Craig's taunting, he said, "Jean nearly bankrupted us buying them, and they're uglier than ——." (I won't tell you what word goes in the blank, but I bet you can guess.)

As if that weren't humiliating enough, Craig added, "So your wife collects dolls, eh? You need to knock her up, Rick. Or at least give her a good reaming."

You can see why I got so mad. What does collecting dolls have to do with not having children or not making whoopee? It's narrow-minded, juvenile people like Craig who make life hard for all the nice people! I almost charged into the living room to give Craig a piece of my mind, but I bit my tongue. I didn't want to get upset right before the other guests arrived.

Well, as it turned out, I didn't have much to worry about, because of the eight people I invited, only three showed up: my friend Patti the creative writing teacher and two of my co-workers, Sharon and Fulgencio. I felt really sorry for Fulgencio as I served the cucumber and cream cheese hors d'oeuvres, because Craig and Rick kept making these veiled cracks about his name and accent. Rick had decided that Fulgencio (who is from Mexico) is, well, not all that masculine, just because he's small-statured and graduated from a fashion-design school on the West Coast. It goes back to what I said earlier about making fun of people for things they can't

control. Is it Fulgencio's fault that he's not from this country?

Rick and Craig kept up their antics during the serving of the main course. Now, I had spent hours preparing more than a dozen game hens, but did they appreciate it? Nooo! "What the hell is this?" Rick bellowed. At least Craig put a little more creativity into his insult: "I never knew sparrow could taste so good."

> **"'What the hell is this?' Rick bellowed. At least Craig put a little more creativity into his insult: 'I never knew sparrow could taste so good.'"**

Well, despite all the bad stuff that had happened, I thought dessert would more than make up for it: Chocolate Fudge Marble Upside-Down Baked Alaska with cherry flambé topping! My masterpiece! I had Patti turn down the lights as I carried the flaming dessert into the dining room.

"Well, would you look at this," Rick said. "Jean thinks she's Martha Stewart."

"Yeah," Craig replied, "about two hundred pounds later."

That did it. I put the dessert down on the table and marched to our bedroom, where the guests' coats were being kept. My plan was to snatch Craig's down vest, return to the dining room, throw it over his head, and order him to leave. (And Rick could go with him!) But something happened before I got the chance.

What follows is the hardest thing I've ever had to write. Even harder than the tribute I wrote to Princess Di after her death.

For you see, when I opened the bedroom door, I found my kitty, Arthur, sprawled out on the floor in an unnatural way. I rushed over to him and noticed that something was protruding from his mouth.

Arthur had choked to death on my Pinchers The Lobster Teenie Beanie Baby.

Well, after that, the dinner party just fell apart. About five minutes later, Patti came into the bedroom, concerned that I hadn't returned. When she saw what had happened, she ran and got Rick and Craig.

"Sorry about your cat," Craig said. "You want me and Rick to go bury it somewhere? I got a shovel in my pickup."

I guess I was not in my right mind at the time, because I agreed. I got an old narrow box out of my closet and laid Arthur in it. I couldn't quite pry the Teenie Beanie Baby out of his mouth, because his jaws had stiffened, so I decided to let it be.

"'Sorry about your cat,' Craig said. 'You want me and Rick to go bury it somewhere? I got a shovel in my pickup.'"

Rick and Craig were gone a lot longer than was necessary. Finally, at about 2 a.m., Rick arrived home, smelling like a brewery. I asked him what he had done with Arthur.

"The ground was too hard to bury the cat," Rick said, "so we drove around for a while and tossed it in a dumpster behind the Old Country Buffet. Here's your box back."

Well, you can be sure I gave hubby Rick the biggest tongue-lashing of our whole marriage. Like I said, I wasn't in my right mind, and I said a lot of things I probably shouldn't have said, like how he never liked Arthur anyway, and how he didn't care at all how I felt, and how he was so insensitive, and how he could never say anything without being vulgar. Then I went into our bedroom, slammed the door, threw myself on the bed, and bawled for almost two hours.

As I said, this won't be the merriest of Christmases in the Teasdale household. But I am coping, and, thank God, I still have my other kitty, Priscilla. On my friend Patti's advice, I'm trying to work out my grief through my writing. So I wrote a poem about Arthur that I would like to share with you:

Arthur, you left us all too soon,

But for me it was eight years of joy.

You were not always appreciated during your short life, it's true.

(One person I won't name would have preferred a chocolate lab.)

But I understood your beauty, your magic, your sweetness. I hope that Jesus is playing with you up in Heaven above,

Dangling your Cat Dancer toy that you loved so much.

(That is, until you put on all that weight a few years ago.)

It is tragic when a mother outlives her children,

But I will remember you always.

I used to say that when I got to Heaven,

The first person I wanted to see was my grandmother.

But I have to change that now, my sweet little Arthur. ✐

Holiday Travel Plans

How will *you* be dealing with hectic holiday travel?

Billy Tetreault
Marketing advisor

"I'll be the guy on the bus with Bing Crosby's *White Christmas* blaring from my boombox, which I will carry on my shoulder."

Caroline Stroli
Teacher

"I'm converting to Islam. Not only will I do my holiday traveling in a different month, I won't have to visit my family since they'll disown me!"

Lonny Werner
Buzzsaw Operator

"I'll be glued to the Weather Channel for inclement weather and traffic reports so I know how anxious to be when I travel."

Vacationing Woman Thinks Cats Miss Her

VERO BEACH, FL—Annette Davrian, a 45-year-old Cedar Rapids, IA, bank teller, is spending her vacation time in a delusional haze this week, somehow managing to convince herself that her cats actually miss her.

"Buttons is so sensitive, I just know she's scared and frightened without her Mommy by her side," Davrian told uninterested relatives Monday, just hours after arriving in Florida. "And Bonkers gets so cranky when he doesn't get his morning treats. I hope they'll be able to handle this emotionally. I've always gone to great lengths to assure them that they're loved, but they've never been left alone this long before. If they think I've abandoned them, I'd never be able to forgive myself."

Animal behaviorists agree that cats are incapable of feeling sadness over an owner's absence, asserting that their only reaction to such an event would be a brief adjustment period to claim household territory previously thought to be the owner's.

Davrian, who has lived alone since the death of her mother nine years ago, has considered cutting her vacation short because of the cats' nonexistent longing for her to return.

> ## "'I just dump some Purina in the bowl, and I'm gone. And do the cats give a shit? No, they do not. Why? Because they're cats.'"

"Those poor, precious kitties," she told a man in an elevator. "I'm all they've got in this world. What will they do without me?"

According to coworker Phil Gross, Davrian began worrying about her cats' imaginary sadness over her Florida trip nearly three weeks before leaving. On Dec. 10, Davrian expressed concern to Gross that the cats might not sufficiently "bond" with a stranger entrusted with their care. Based on this worry alone, she delayed her trip for two weeks, paying a large rescheduling fee for her plane ticket.

"She asked me to look after the cats while she was gone," neighbor Janet Pull-

Annette Davrian with cat Bonkers

man said. "I said sure, figuring I'd just have to feed them. Turns out, she wanted me to go in there three times a day and stay at least 20 minutes each time so the cats would feel 'adequately socialized.' Then she hands me a list of things to do that's, like, 40 items long."

""The thing just sits in the window and watches birds all day, just the way it did before she left, and just the way it'll keep on doing after she gets back, every day until one of the two of them dies.'"

Pullman admitted that she has not followed the elaborate instructions, merely filling up the cats' food and water bowls when they are empty.

"I just dump some Purina in the bowl, and I'm gone," Pullman said. "And do the cats give a shit? No, they do not. Why? Because they're cats."

Hoping to ease the pain and loneliness of her asocial, predatory pets, Davrian has left numerous long messages on her answering machine, claiming that the cats will appreciate hearing her voice. She also wrapped one of her sweaters around a pillow before leaving so Buttons and Bonkers would 'have a bit of me to snuggle with,' unaware that the cats' motivation for 'snuggling' is to maintain body temperature, not to feel emotionally connected to their food provider.

As a supplement to the answering-machine messages, Davrian left the clock radio playing in the bathroom "to keep the little ones company." Though the cats could not care less about the radio, the same cannot be said of neighbor Bob Franz, 49, whose bathroom shares a heating vent with Davrian's.

"I once heard [Davrian] say that [Bonkers] will get lonely without a human voice around to make him feel reassured," Franz said. "But the thing just sits in the window and watches birds all day, just the way it did before she left, and just the way it'll keep on doing after she gets back, every day until one of the two of them dies. Meantime, the damn radio yabbers on all day and night. That radio's probably more aware that the woman's gone than Bonkers."

The Florida excursion is not the first time Davrian has ruined her leisure time fretting about the cats. Since 1996, she has failed to enjoy 219 activities or excursions, including two trips to Lake Winnepesaukee, a visit to a local botanical garden, 23 movies, and three dinners—each of which she spent worrying about being "out of phone contact in case something goes wrong."

Davrian could not be reached for additional comment, as she had just cut short a sailing trip in order to, as brother-in-law Don Koechley said, "make sure the damn cats are okay." Ø

Your Horoscope

The stars agree—you're getting way too old for all of this shit.

- **Aries** Crackling with the warmth of the season, a yuletide fire will quickly consume your helpless flesh.

- **Taurus** An attempt to concentrate on more intellectual pursuits will ultimately fail this week, thanks to that shiny thing over there.

- **Gemini** Though not a mood ring by design, your wedding band will soon communicate the misery and hopelessness you feel inside.

- **Cancer** You'll be brought to your knees this Thursday by nothing more than a severe and irreversible case of gangrene.

- **Leo** While you've reasoned your way out of tricky situations before, a crisis this week involving a fox, a chicken, and a bag of feed will leave you completely stumped.

- **Virgo** You've never been the type to ask for help. Sadly, though, you've always been the type to beg for it.

- **Libra** An engrossing read will soon transport you to a strange and faraway land, leaving you stranded in Harlem after 30 missed stops.

- **Scorpio** Your lucky 19th-century German-language philosophers for this week are: Heidegger, Nietzsche, Schopenhauer, and Wundt.

- **Sagittarius** The National Institute Of Raised Expectations Followed By Disappointing Results will come very close to honoring you this week.

- **Capricorn** You never thought having a kid could be so exhausting, but then staying one step ahead of Child Protective Services does take its toll.

- **Aquarius** The rise of Venus in your sign can only mean one thing: This will be a great week to read too much into stuff.

- **Pisces** Speak directly from the heart this week. Tell your loved one, "Re-circulate the blood! Re-circulate the blood! Re-circulate the blood!"

Religious Cousin Ruins Family's Christmas

MONTOURSVILLE, PA—The arrival of devout Christian cousin Barb Krueger has "for all practical purposes ruined" the Langan family's chances of having an enjoyable holiday season, sources reported Monday.

"Christmas Day is something our whole family greatly looks forward to, drinking eggnog, opening presents, sitting around the family room in our pajamas and robes, and sipping hot cocoa throughout the day," said Marv Langan, 51. "Well, you can forget about that this year, with Barb hovering over us with her Bible."

The Langans have for years treasured Christmas as a time for family bonding and good cheer. But all that is likely to change this year due to the presence of Krueger, 30, who describes herself as having "a deeply committed personal relationship with my Lord and Savior, Jesus Christ."

"Jesus is the reason for the season," Krueger said.

The Langan family struggles to enjoy the holiday season despite their guest.

> **"'The first thing she did when she got here was explain that our Christmas tree was a pagan tradition Jesus never would have approved of.'"**

The trouble began for the Langans in early December, when the family was contacted by Krueger, who explained that she was in the Montoursville area for a six-week Bible-study program and looking for a place to spend the holidays. The Langans, who readily welcomed the visiting cousin into their home, were unaware that she had spent a majority of her adult life attending various "personal enrichment programs," converting to a conservative synod of the Lutheran church and gradually alienating all non-Christian members of her social circle.

"The first thing she did when she got here was explain that our Christmas tree was a pagan tradition Jesus never would have approved of," said mother Janet Langan, 49. "Not long after, she nearly fainted when she discovered we didn't have an Advent calendar in the house, so Marv had to run out and buy one."

With Krueger's arrival came other changes, as well. The Langans, who belong to Montoursville's Holy Christ Almighty Church but attend services just a few times a year, soon found themselves roped into twice-weekly visits.

"Last Thursday night, I'd just baked a pie, and the whole gang was getting ready

---

"'She says Jesus teaches us to love the sinner and condemn the sin, but I hate her.'"

---

to go sledding together," Janet said. "Next thing you know, Barb is asking about Advent services. I'd forgotten that there was such a thing. Well, there was no sledding that night, let me tell you."

Other holiday-cheer-killing activities foisted upon the family include daily "devotionals" involving candle-lighting and scripture readings, formal prayers before all meals, and longwinded harangues explaining why Jesus wants the Langans to reject such "blasphemously secular" holiday TV specials as *Frosty*

The Snowman and *Rudolph The Red-Nosed Reindeer.*

"Caroling is usually my favorite thing," 8-year-old Justin Langan said. "But Cousin Barb says we shouldn't sing Santa songs. All she likes is stupid, hard-to-sing, religious stuff about Good King Wenceslaus and Feast of Stephen—crap like that."

According to daughter Brianna Langan, 17, the family's annual trip to see Santa Claus at the local mall was "a complete wash-out" because of Krueger.

"It totally sucked this year," Brianna said. "The whole time, everybody just stood there all quiet, glancing back at Cousin Barb, worried about what she would think." Brianna added that while waiting in line to see Santa, her visiting cousin told her she shouldn't be wearing makeup at her age.

"I didn't talk to one boy the whole time we were at the mall," said Michelle Langan, Brianna's 15-year-old sister. "Every time I saw somebody I knew from school, Cousin Barb just glared at them and scared them off. She says Jesus teaches us to love the sinner and condemn the sin, but I hate her."

"I hope she never comes back here again," Michelle continued. "I hope she gets run over by a bus and goes to Heaven. That way, she could spend the holidays with her best friend Jesus." *Ø*

Poor Kwanzaa Sales Disappoint Retailers

WASHINGTON, DC—Kwanzaa officials received sobering news Monday, as the Department of Commerce announced that Kwanzaa holiday sales for the U.S. totalled $178. The figure represents the lowest total since 1992, the year the holiday was invented. At Abe's Kwanzaa Emporium in Los Angeles, rows of unsold Kwanzaa trees were thrown out, while rolls of Kwanzaa-themed wrapping paper gathered dust in giant bins. Even A&M Records' much-hyped holiday CD, *A Bryan Adams Kwanzaa*, fared poorly, selling just three copies.

Weed Delivery Guy Saves Christmas

MADISON, WI—The holidays evoke images of carolers and hot cocoa, sleigh rides through the crisp country air, and chestnuts roasting on an open fire. But for the four residents of a drafty little apartment on Johnson Street, such holiday traditions seemed nothing more than fairy tales. For, through a combination of poverty, circumstance, and plain old bad luck, these young gentlemen nearly saw their holiday dreams shattered like so many fallen ornaments.

Almost, but not quite. For although there would be no yule log in the fireplace, a crackling blaze of another kind would come to warm the hearts of the hapless roommates. For, these four lucky friends had a guardian angel watching over them, and this is the heartwarming true story of how the weed delivery guy saved Christmas.

"Dude, I was so bummed when I found out my stupid supervisor scheduled me for first shift Christmas Eve," said Patrick Moynihan, 26, a "part-time musician and full-time phone drone." "I was like, 'Come on, I gotta go to Milwaukee to see my old man and watch the game.' He was like, 'Sorry man, life's rough. You should've remembered to ask off.'"

"It's not like Milwaukee's so great," Moynihan added, "but it beats spending Christmas alone in my shithole apartment."

But, in a turn of events Moynihan described as "X-Files-type shit," each of his remaining roommates—first Dirk, then Kleist, and finally even White Jimmy—watched their Christmas plans come undone, leaving

The weed guy delivers holiday tidings.

the four housemates together in Madison on the night before Christmas.

"I was supposed to go home with this chick and meet her parents," said Dirk Udell, 24, a part-time bicycle-store clerk and bassist. "But we totally got into this huge fight the night before, and she was like, 'Sayonara, sweetheart.' Then Kleist got wasted and slept through his flight, and White Jimmy's credit card got turned down at the bus station, because he maxed it out on that amp he bought."

Individual heartbreak turned into collective joy when the roommates realized that they could have their own Christmas... together.

"We said, 'Fuck it,'" James "White Jimmy" Gaines said. "We were like, 'We have all the ingredients for old-time holiday cheer right here: some brews, the tube, and the Chinese place across the street that never closes on holidays.' We even cleaned the living room and washed the dishes. Then fate threw a monkey wrench."

> "Individual heartbreak turned into collective joy when the roommates realized that they could have their own Christmas. . .together."

"Dudes, it's a no go," Kleist said before delivering the bad news. "Carl totally flaked on us. He left for Michigan already."

The roommates' faces turned ashen: There would be no Christmas weed.

"I was, like, 'No way, man!'" Moynihan said. "Kleist even called all our friends, trying to find someone who was holding, but everyone was out of town. We tried to drum up some Christmas cheer, but there was no escaping the sad reality that the four of us had all this time to hang out, but no pot."

Disconsolate, the roommates went through the motions of scraping the bowl for resin. But, in their hearts, they knew that it wasn't enough to get them high. Peering out of the fourth-floor window, gazing at the municipal streetlight decorations below, they felt that Christmas had deserted them... Or had it?

The residents of Apt. 4-D celebrate Christmas together.

"That's when Jimmy—I think it was Jimmy. It could've been Kleist—wait, was it Jimmy or Kleist?" Moynihan said. "Aw, never mind—whoever it was looked up and said, 'Hey Dirk, why don't we try the number that that guy who worked at Big Mike's Subs gave you?'"

After searching high and low with the help of his three determined roommates, Udell located the piece of paper containing the phone number given to him by his old stoner buddy Javier.

"Javier told me he hardly knows the dealer, but the guy always has really great shit and he comes right over," Udell said. "Kleist was all like, 'Who in their right mind is gonna be out delivering weed on Christmas Eve?' But I was like, 'What would it hurt to give the number a try?'"

"We were so psyched when he answered his cell on the second ring!" Udell added.

The roommates busily prepared for the weed guy's arrival by laying out Chips Ahoy cookies on paper plates, loading disks into the CD changer, and lovingly placing a new screen in the bong. All the while, they listened for the crunch-crunch-crunch of his footsteps on the snowy walk and the jingle-jangle-jingle of the Apt. 4-D buzzer. They even put the porch light on for the dude, so he'd feel welcome. And when, in less than an hour, the weed delivery guy showed up bearing a gift more precious than gold, the roommates' hearts soared with joy.

"That stranger brought us something so much better than any store-bought gift," Moynihan said. "I don't know his name—it's considered bad form to ask—but he taught us that Christmas wishes can come true, if you believe."

And so it was that the weed delivery guy—hardworking, dedicated, and discreet—saved Christmas in the nick of time.

"We may not have had a big tree and all that," Moynihan said. "And there wasn't eggnog dusted with nutmeg, 'cause the only time we ever had any nutmeg in the house was the time we tried to trip on it. Not recommended, by the way. But we had a happy Christmas all the same."

It wasn't long before all through the house, not a creature was stirring up off the couch. The boys opened the baggie and packed a bowl with delight, murmuring, "Happy Christmas, weed delivery guy. You did us one right." *Ø*

Dad's Marine Corps Training Evident During Christmas-Present Opening

CHARLESTON, SC—Retired Cpl. Kent Packard, 58, rarely puts his Marine Corps expertise to use, except during the yearly Christmas gift exchange, family sources reported Monday. "Every year, exactly two hours after cutting the ham, Dad makes us line up by the tree, then he distributes the presents to us in increasing order of age," his 17-year-old son Jerome said. "When he unwraps his own gifts, he lines up the pieces of cardboard and plastic packaging in a neat row, like he's field-stripping a rifle." Although family members say they admire Packard's acumen, they've warned him against waking the house with a Christmas-morning bugle rendition of "Jingle Bells."

It's Christmas Time—And I'm In A Holi-Daze!

'Twas the weeks before Christmas,

And all through my home,

Until my kids get some presents

They won't leave me alone!

Write On The Funny!
By Roger Dudek

Well, folks, it's that time of year again. The time when we all gather round the fireplace to celebrate the miraculous birth of a child that happened over 2,000 years ago. No, I'm not talking about Andy Rooney! I'm talking about Christmas—and you know what *that* means:

Run for your lives! The fruitcakes are coming!

Now, if you're a loyal reader (This week's Tip of the *Santa's* Hat goes to Ann Marie Ganz of Portage, MI!) you know I've never been too nuts (or fruits) about fruitcake. But honestly, who is? The last time anyone actually took a bite of a fruitcake was 1952, and I should know—it's still sitting on my mother's kitchen table with a fork stuck in it. It was there so long she finally had to put it in her will…as the thing that probably killed her! Talk about a *recipe for disaster.* This one takes the cake!

But seriously, folks, if the mailman tries to bring one of those things to my door this year, I'll be spending Christmas in prison for assault with a deadly confection.

Turns out waking up to something that's about as crusty, old, and stale as Keith Richards is the *least* of my worries this holiday season. (Did someone say, "I Can't Get No Fruit-Filled-Confection?") With only a few shopping days left before the dreaded 25th, it's time to hit the stores! Best Buy, Target, Toys "R" Too-Expensive-for-You-to-Afford…they're like loony bins filled with crazy parents fighting over the one hot item everyone's trying to snatch up first: a parking space! You guys know what I'm talking about. The last time I saw this many grown adults fighting over a piece of concrete, it was dividing Berlin!

Parking lot? More like parking little, if you ask me.

> **"Best Buy, Target, Toys "R" Too-Expensive-for-You-to-Afford…they're like loony bins filled with crazy parents fighting over the one hot item everyone's trying to snatch up first: a parking space! You guys know what I'm talking about."**

Even if I do get a space, I don't have a clue what to buy once I get inside. Bicycles and digital cameras and DVDs—oh my! It's all about video games this year, and my kids are starting to sound like little piglets: "Wii, Wii, Wii!"

I told them they'd be getting a Wii for

"Unless I make a break for the North Pole, the only reindeer I'll be seeing this holiday season is Uncle Howard getting *Blitzen.* *Silent Night*? Holy Hangover! Oh, I *sleigh* me!"

Christmas...just as soon as I win the loterii (lottery)!

Whatever happened to waking up Christmas morning to a new sled and a pair of tube socks? The only "video game" I remember playing in my youth was trying to hit "record" on the VCR right at the beginning of *It's A Wonderful Life.* "Every time a bell rings an angel gets its wings." And every time *four* bells ring it's one of my kids calling me with another battery-operated doohickey to add to the list! I'm telling you, they're getting so demanding, it's practically *ex-toy-rtion*!

Now, call me the Grinch, but there's a better chance of an embryo attaching itself to my wife's hostile uterine lining than there is of me heading down to the Costco to spend a week's pay on some souped-up Atari nonsense. The only *Resident Evil* that's coming into this house on Christmas is Aunt Judy's Waldorf salad!

And speaking of family, what would Christmas be without a visit from the relatives? I'll tell you what...*happy*! My whole family in the same place at once? Ho, Ho, Holy smokes, I gotta get out of here! Christmas morning's going to be a sugarplum *nightmare*! No, but seriously, why doesn't somebody just hit me with a *yule log* right in the *eggnog*-gin, because unless I make a break for the North Pole, the only reindeer I'll be seeing this holiday season is my Uncle Howard getting *Blitzen. Silent Night*? Holy Hangover!

Oh, I *sleigh* me!

I guess there's nothing left to do but hang my stockings, eat some Christmas cookies, and wait patiently for the night when my house will be visited by a fat, bearded stranger who lives up north and has been secretly watching me all year.

But enough about my mother-in-law! Merry Christmas! *∅*

Important Christmas Lessons Already Forgotten

HARTFORD, CT—As the nation moves on from last month's family gatherings, churchgoing, and goodwill toward men, the annual post-Christmas readjustment process is proceeding on schedule, with millions of Americans forgoing their temporary generosity of spirit and resuming their petty, miserable treatment of one another.

Though the joy and glad tidings of the holiday season are mere weeks behind us, sources report that more than 85 percent of 1999's Christmastime lessons have already been forgotten, with that number expected to reach 98 percent by as early as next week.

> "Children who learned the important lesson that it is better to give than receive are refusing to share their expensive new toys with less fortunate playmates, gloating over their possessions, and berating the other children for being poor."

"Christmas is a magical time of year when people of all ages and backgrounds put aside their differences and are reminded of the things that truly count: the joy of giving, the gleam in a young child's eye, and the sound of voices raised together in song," said James Samuelson of the Hartford-based Institute For American Cultural Mores & Values, which tracks the rise and fall of human love and kindness throughout the year. "Mid-January to early February, by contrast, is a magical time of year when people forget all about that stuff. This leads to mid- to late February, a magical time of year when people everywhere feel overpowering, soul-crushing emotional pain, causing them to hate their coworkers, their loved ones, and themselves."

Evidence of this phenomenon can be seen across the country, with Christmas miracles of universal benevolence and spiritual uplift degenerating into mid-January miracles of everyday banality and neglect. Corporations that donated generously to the homeless and various charities mere weeks ago have resumed their usual cutthroat, profit-driven practices. Children who learned the important lesson that it is better to give than receive are refusing to share their expensive new toys with less fortunate playmates, gloating over their possessions, and berating the other children for being poor. And the many career-focused dads who made a major breakthrough during the holiday season, vowing to spend quality time with their wives and children, are systematically unlearning these realizations of what truly matters and returning to their dysfunctional workaholic patterns.

"I hadn't seen my ailing grandmother, who just turned 91 and lives all alone out in Arizona, in over three years," said Boston investment banker Carl Thompson on Dec. 27. "But then, the wife and I, along with several other members of our church, went caroling at the homes of various elderly shut-ins as part of our holiday outreach program. As I looked into the eyes of those poor souls, so happy to have visitors on this blustery winter evening, I learned a valuable lesson about life, about family, and about myself. It was hard to book a flight out to Phoenix at the last minute, but just when it looked like there were no seats left, a reservation was canceled, and I made it out there to visit Grandma in time for Christmas Eve. It was a Christmas miracle. I know that God wanted me to be on that plane."

When asked about his grandmother again Tuesday, Thompson said, "That old bag? Christ, she didn't call again, did she? Does she think the world revolves around her and her stupid heart-medication stories she drones on and on about all day and night? Jesus, I'm a busy man here."

Janice Frye, 34, a Los Angeles single mother, related a similarly moving story on Dec. 29.

"My 6-year-old son Brandon is a real handful, suffering from hyperactivity and a whole host of emotional problems. Sometimes the stress of taking care of him all by myself is just too much. But then, when I think of the little baby Jesus lying in the manger, I realize how special and wonderful Brandon really is. On Christmas Eve,

when he gave me a drawing he made that said, 'I Love Mommy,' I knew he is the one true light of my life."

> ## "'If everybody behaved so kindly to one another all year round, Christmas wouldn't seem special at all."

Less than two weeks later, the screaming and dish-throwing that typifies Frye's emotionally abusive relationship with her child had resumed. Neighbors reported overhearing Frye yell, "I should have had you aborted," and the child's antisocial

A Christmas tree, symbol of "the most special time of the year," lies discarded in a Norfolk, VA, alley.

behavior and poor performance in school have worsened.

Such forgetting-the-Christmas-spirit stories are not uncommon. According to Samuelson, the process is not only normal, but essential to preserving the special feeling associated with the holiday.

"The positive, soul-enriching sentiments associated with the holiday season are shared by almost all Americans, regardless of religious beliefs or cultural backgrounds," Samuelson said. "But it is only through our regular mean-spirited shallowness the rest of the year that the spirit of Christmas can, by contrast, move us so deeply, deluding the populace into thinking their lives are actually beautiful. If everybody behaved so kindly to one another all year round, Christmas wouldn't seem special at all. And then, the magic of Christmas would be lost forever, swallowed up by a year-round sense of basic human decency that would rob the holidays of their warm glow, ruining Christmas for all the little children of the world."

"If you think about it, the eleven and a half months of cruelty, selfishness, and disrespect exhibited by nearly all of humanity may, in fact, be the most precious gift of all," he added, wiping a tear from his eye. "It is this non-holy miracle of man's non-holiday inhumanity to man that is the true meaning of Christmas." Ø

Natalee Holloway Makes New Year's Resolution To Become Famous

BIRMINGHAM, AL—At a quiet New Year's Eve party with friends, Mountain Brook High School senior Natalee Holloway made a resolution to be famous before the end of the calendar year. "I may just be an 18-year-old with my whole life ahead of me, but mark my words, I'm going to capture the public's attention in a big way," Holloway said. "I don't need to be rich, powerful, smart, or important—I just want to be famous. And I would like to use my fame to help others become famous—people like Nancy Grace, who is sadly underutilized on her sole program, Court TV's *Closing Arguments*." Holloway's mother Beth Twitty immediately joined in with a resolution of her own to tirelessly bolster her daughter's fame "on every news magazine show" if she has to.

Prescription Put In 2009 New Year's Eve Glasses

Nation Struggles To Understand Why Area Pie Didn't Come Out Right

HASTINGS, NE—Citizens across the nation were shocked and dismayed Thursday when a pie, originally intended to be a delectable, mouthwatering treat, somehow emerged from the oven in less-than-ideal condition.

The disappointing dessert—a cranberry-apple pie baked by Hastings woman Cathy Stanger—was described by those who tried it as gooey and saccharine, with a slightly bitter aftertaste, and has left a baffled nation struggling to understand how a pie that should have been so delicious could go so wrong.

"It...it just doesn't make any sense," Phoenix construction worker Dale Wallace said. "The crust was brown. Not a light golden brown, but dark brown. Almost black. There was no tartness in the filling, and the bottom was mushy. It wasn't flaky or succulent, either. How could this have happened?"

In a desperate search for answers, some Americans have directly called into question Stanger's methods in preparing the lackluster baked good.

Specific criticisms include Stanger's choice of fruits, with many saying that

What should have been a scrumptious baked good.

perhaps a Granny Smith or Golden Delicious apple should have been used instead of Honeycrisp. Other detractors have suggested that Stanger should never have strayed from pumpkin, which is generally acknowledged to be her signature pie.

"She probably didn't follow all the directions," Orlando, FL, resident Vivian Werner said. "Sometimes, you just miss a step somewhere along the way or figure you can wing it. Obviously, mistakes were made, and now the whole nation is paying the price."

"You know what, I bet she overcooked it," Werner continued. "People always leave pies in too long. I have no idea why."

> "'You know what, I bet she overcooked it. People always leave pies in too long. I have no idea why.'"

> "Other detractors have suggested that Stanger should never have strayed from pumpkin, which is generally acknowledged to be her signature pie."

A Rasmussen poll found that 37 percent of Americans surveyed thought that Stanger had probably added too much salt to the crust, 24 percent believed that maybe she used an off-brand of cornstarch in the pie filling, 16 percent speculated that her oven might have some hot spots, and 7 percent felt that the pie was probably not that bad if you popped it in the microwave with a little scoop of ice cream on top.

Official reaction to the pie has been swift and decisive. Rep. Ben Chandler (D-KY) took to the floor of the House to denounce the pie as unappealing, within hours of its removal from the oven. Later that afternoon, the Senate convened a special investigative panel to determine what went wrong with the pie and plans to release its report in June of next year.

In the meantime, President Barack Obama attempted to soothe the nation in his weekly video address.

"My fellow Americans, we are all discouraged by the outcome of the pie in Hastings," Obama said. "It was meant to feed six people, with leftovers for lunch the next day. But what's important now is that we have our best minds working on the Hastings pie, studying it, analyzing it. Making sure that something like this never happens again. Rest assured, there will be more pies."

"And in a personal message to Cathy Stanger: Did you remember to cover the edge of the crust with foil?" Obama continued. "You should try that next time. It keeps the crust from burning."∅

Ho! Ho! Ho! I Am God

Ho! Ho! Ho! Seasons greetings, boys and girls. It's almost time for Christmas. I'll bet you can't wait, eh? I thought so! Ho! Ho! Ho! You just love Christmas, don't you? Oh, so do I. Ho! Ho! Ho! I love visiting each and every one of your homes, stuffing your stockings with toys, and enjoying the milk and cookies you leave for me. But mostly I love Christmas because it's the celebration of the birth of my only son, Jesus the Christ. You see, I'm God.

The True Meaning Of Christmas
By Santa Claus

Oh, don't look at me funny. I want to see you smile. Smile for Santa! Come on. If you don't smile, I won't give you what you want for Christmas this year. Oh, there we go! Ho! Ho! Ho! That's a good child. Now bring your little ear close to Santa. I want to tell you something. A little closer. There we are. If you're very, very good this year, I'm going to give you everlasting life in my heavenly kingdom. Would you like that? Oh, I'll bet you would! Ho! Ho! Ho!

You probably think you only see me at Christmas time, don't you? Well, that's not true. You see me every Sunday in church. Look at me. Don't I look familiar to you? I'm old, I have a while beard, I love everyone. I'm the same God as the one you and your mommy and daddy worship on Sundays.

You do know why I want you to be on my list of good boys and girls, don't you? Why I don't want you to tell lies, or be disrespectful to your parents? Of course you do. Because those are my Ten Commandments, the ones I emblazoned onto stone tablets and handed down the mount to Moses thousands of years ago. And when you obey my Ten Commandments, I reward you with lovely presents, such as eternal life. If you disobey them, I punish you with the searing fires of Hell. That's what a God does. But you've been good, haven't you? Of course you have! Ho! Ho! Ho! You're all such good boys and girls. Santa loves you.

> "You probably think you only see me at Christmas time, don't you? Well, that's not true. You see me every Sunday in church. Look at me. Don't I look familiar to you? I'm old, I have a white beard, I love everyone."

Oh, but sometimes Santa gets sad. Yes, I do. Do you know why? Because I don't have anything to do all year except on Christmas Eve. Well, except for listening to all the precious prayers of you good little boys and girls, of course. I listen to all your prayers all year 'round. I listen to your parents' prayers, too. And then, when Christmas approaches, my elves—oops! I mean, my angels—and I work very hard building all the toys. I have many angels, with mighty wings and flowing robes as bright as the sun.

I try to stay jolly. Because what kind of Santa would I be if I weren't jolly? Not much of one, that's for sure! Ho! Ho! Ho! But it's not easy being God. It's very cold on the North Pole—Heaven. I live in Heaven, of course. It's always warm up there, and we listen to beautiful harp music all the livelong day.

Okay, I admit it. I'm not God. But I'm better than God. I'm jollier, and I give you real toys, not boring old psalms and empty promises you can only collect on when you die. Worship me, not him! Worship Santa! I am God! 🍃

NEWS IN PHOTOS

Baby New Year Abandoned In Street

Mom Brought To Tears By Thing Picked Up At Airport

COLUMBIA, MO—Joan Hadler, a Columbia-area mother of three, wept tears of joy Monday over a cheap, last-minute present her visiting son Troy bought at an airport gift shop en route home.

The inexpensive teapot Troy purchased as an afterthought.

"I had a layover in St. Louis and had about an hour to kill. There was a gift shop called 'That's Something Else' in the C Concourse, so I figured, 'Hey, I should pick up something for Mom,'" said Troy Hadler, 25, who now lives in Alexandria, VA. "I picked her up this little teapot, and when I gave it to her, she was so touched, there were tears running down her face. I was glad she liked it, but she liked it so much, I kind of felt sorry for her."

Upon being handed the gift, wrapped only in a plastic bag, Joan protested that her son's visit home was "all the present [she] needed." After opening the bag and seeing the teapot, however, her eyes welled up with tears, and she hugged Troy repeatedly.

"Mom cradled it in her arms like it was a Fabergé egg," Troy said. "It made her so incredibly happy. I guess I made the right decision when I chose it over the pewter replica of the St. Louis Arch."

Though Troy said he loves his mother "very much," he admitted that he rarely buys her gifts. On Monday, however, he went the extra mile and spent approximately 60 seconds picking out the $29 flowered enameled teapot.

> "'I know Mom wasn't trying to make me feel guilty by overreacting. She genuinely did love it. Just like she loved the Washington, DC, sweatshirt I got her last year and the Blue Mountain e-card I sent her on her birthday in 1999.'"

"I'm sure it was stupid to get something like that at an airport," Hadler said. "It's obviously just some overpriced, crappy version of an actually nice teapot, but I wasn't about to run all over St. Louis comparison-shopping for teapots."

Compounding Troy's guilt, his overjoyed mother told him that the teapot would have "a place of honor" among the decorative teacups she displays in her home's dining-room cabinet.

"Maybe I subconsciously knew she collected teacups and that's why I got it, but that's unlikely," Troy said. "Pretty much, I was just looking around and saw the teapot and thought, 'Hey, I think mom drinks tea.'"

Despite Troy's insistence that the gift was "no biggie," his mother continued to treat it as a special event well into the next day.

Said next-door neighbor Francine Geis: "I was watering my azalea bushes Tuesday when Joan saw me over the fence. She waved me over and said, 'You've got to come inside and see what Troy brought me all the way from Washington, DC!'"

The neighbor stood by as Joan "oohed and aahed" over the teapot, talking at length about what a thoughtful son she has.

"I wanted to yell, 'Stop! No, I'm not!'" said Troy, who was present for the sad display of unjustified maternal pride. "The only effort I expended in buying the gift was the two-second struggle I had trying to pull the credit card out of my wallet."

"I know Mom wasn't trying to make me feel guilty by overreacting," Troy continued. "She genuinely did love it. Just like she loved the Washington, DC, sweatshirt I got her last year and the Blue Mountain e-card I sent her on her birthday in 1999."

To assuage his guilt, Troy has made a pact with himself to buy his mother "a nice necklace or something" from a non-airport gift shop the next time he visits.

"I've got to get her a gift that's actually decent next time," Troy said. "The look of joy on her face from that crappy teapot, man, I felt like the worst son in the whole world."

"Mom said she'd think of me whenever she used the teapot," Troy added. "In turn, I guess I'll think of her whenever I'm in an airport gift shop." ⍝

Book Given As Gift Actually Read

LONG BEACH, CA—The nation's publishing industry was rocked by Monday's news that a book given as a holiday gift was actually read and enjoyed by its recipient. According to reports, Long Beach schoolteacher Gavin Wallace completed *James Gleick's Genius: The Life And Science Of Richard Feynman*, a present from his cousin. "I was very interested in Dr. Feynman, after having seen a TV show on him last month," Wallace told reporters. "So, having some time to myself over the holidays, I read the book, which I enjoyed thoroughly." Wallace previously made headlines for his December 1996 consumption of the entire contents of a Hickory Farms gift basket.

Survival of Autoerotic Asphyxiation Closest Thing Man Got To Christmas Miracle

DUNDEE, IL—Amid the hustle and bustle of the holiday season, sometimes there's a little miracle in store for all of us.

And that miracle was more or less what Dundee resident Herb Fosbeck received this past Christmas, when the 38-year-old survived a near-fatal session of oxygen-deprived masturbation.

"The doctors told me I'm lucky to be alive," said Fosbeck, who almost suffocated to death after tying a belt to the base of his showerhead, wrapping the leather strap around his throat, and cutting off his body's circulation in order to heighten climax.

Added Fosbeck, "Somebody up there must sort of like me."

At first glance, the overweight and single Fosbeck might not seem like the kind of character you'd normally see in a heart-warming Christmas tale. And, basically, he isn't, because this is not exactly that type of story. On the other hand, Fosbeck did learn something about the true spirit of the season, albeit in a rather disturbing way. And he didn't die. So if you think about the whole thing with that in mind, it's almost hopeful.

"This is what Christmas is all about, I guess," said police investigator Randy Haverscham, who, along with two other officers and several neighbors, discovered Fosbeck's unconscious body after responding to complaints of a loud crash. "Not really. But still."

A time for hearths, mistletoe, and sharing cider with those you love, Christmas largely passed the solitary Fosbeck by. Not invited to any festive get-togethers, and with no one to curl up with save the hollow-eyed actresses in his vast pornography collection, the middle-aged man's yuletide plans were limited to the fleeting satisfaction of choking himself while tugging weakly at his swollen member.

> **"'This is what Christmas is all about, I guess,' said police investigator Randy Haverscham, who, along with two other officers and several neighbors, discovered Fosbeck's unconscious body after responding to complaints of a loud crash. 'Not really. But still.'"**

As Fosbeck slung the restrictive strap over his head, doing his best to ignore the sounds of carolers outside his open window, did he perhaps think he'd finally hit bottom? We can only assume so. But that turned out not to be the case because, right in the middle of furiously pumping his erection, he slipped in his bathtub, and suddenly found himself spasmodically dangling from his homemade noose.

"I remember putting the belt around my neck, and I guess I must have gotten pretty excited and started moving around too much, because the next thing I knew I was strangling to death," said Fosbeck, who was released from Dundee General Hospital's intensive care ward on Jan. 1. "I don't remember much after that."

"Few could predict that Fosbeck was only moments away from getting the biggest Christmas gift of all. At least, in a just-barely-not-dying-while-tethered-to-a-bathroom-fixture sort of way."

Indeed, few could predict that Fosbeck was only moments away from getting the biggest Christmas gift of all. At least, in a just-barely-not-dying-while-tethered-to-a-bathroom-fixture sort of way.

Using his last gasps of air to scream out for help, the flailing unemployed carpenter suddenly heard in the background the faint jingling of Christmas bells. Was it the arrival of a guardian angel, coming to rescue Fosbeck? Or was it simply an auditory hallucination caused by the lack of oxygen to his brain? We may never know.

One thing, however, remains clear. With a sudden jolt, Fosbeck's showerhead ripped clear from the cheap plaster of his bathroom wall, sending the unconscious loner plummeting free, naked as the baby Jesus.

"He was still tumescent when we found him," said neighbor Bob Ngyuen, who followed police into Fosbeck's apartment. "We put a towel over him before we called the paramedics, just to give him the slightest shred of dignity. It was Christmas, after all."

And if that wasn't enough of a semi-miracle, or miracle-ish thing, or whatever you want to call it, when Fosbeck finally awoke in the hospital, his mother, whom he hadn't seen in four years, was standing over him, re-united with her estranged son on Christmas night.

"The police said I had to come, because they legally can't release a patient with potential brain damage unless they're with a relative or somebody to make sure they get home okay," Elaine Fosbeck, 70, told reporters using her electronic larynx. "Herb was always a disappointment, even as a child."

As Fosbeck looked into the face of his elderly, alcoholic mother, he uttered a familiar phrase, one often used to close holiday stories such as these.

"God bless us, every one," Fosbeck said. "All two of us. Not counting the nurse, who I didn't know." Ø

It Is Not A Wonderful Life

Another miserable year on this dismal rock has come and gone. As for myself, this was one of the worst years I've ever experienced. It was right up there with 1892 and 1921. Among the events of this hateful year: I tried in vain to run away from my estate; I was horrifyingly suckled by a wet-nurse; I received not a single application for my official-mistress position; I was stalked by assassins; and I was assaulted, on separate occasions, by a lowly mule and an automatic enema-dispensing machine. What's more, my hated rival William Randolph Hearst continues to draw breath.

By T. Herman Zweibel, Publisher Emeritus (Photo circa 1911)

There is some-thing else, how-ever, that really sticks in my craw. As everyone knows, I am the richest man in the state, and I own virtually all the property in the village that cringes in the valley below my mountain-top estate. I am also the president and majority stock-holder of the village bank, which has a virtual strangle-hold on the meager finances of the impoverished villagers. I charge such exorbitant interest that the debtor is beholden to me to the grave, and, after his demise, his family must shoulder the remaining debt.

There's a building-and-loan in the village, too, but it has only a fraction of the assets of the bank, and it's always a mere whisper away from insolvency.

Yet, to my great dismay, it somehow manages to stay afloat. If I could just find a way to break this miserable building-and-loan, my conquest would be complete!

There is a soft under-belly of the organization, Uncle Billy, an absent-minded relative of the head-strong young executive secretary who manages it. He's always misplacing important items of business. One day, one of my goons at the bank managed to snatch a large bundle of cash Uncle Billy had laid down, and brought it back to my estate. And all on the same day the bank examiner paid a surprise visit to the building-and-loan!

> **"I am also the president and majority stock-holder of the village bank, which has a virtual strangle-hold on the meager finances of the impoverished villagers. I charge such exorbitant interest that the debtor is beholden to me to the grave, and, after his demise, his family must shoulder the remaining debt."**

Well, I thought this would spell the ruin of the building-and-loan once and for all. The next day, how-ever, Standish informed me that all the villagers had banded together and raised enough money to replace the lost bundle. That young executive secretary must lead a charmed life, or perhaps he has some omnipotent guardian angel.

You can see what kind of a year it has been for me. I should just give up. I would ask Father Christ-mas to bring me a big sack of death, but I am certain I wouldn't get it anyway. 🖋

Beating The Post-Holiday Blahs

Many people report feelings of depression after the holidays. Here are some ways you can relieve the seasonal doldrums:

- Coptic and Greek Orthodox Christians celebrate most holidays days or weeks later. Try temporarily converting to extend your holiday mood.

- Get a full-spectrum light and keep it in your closet. The fact that you know it's there and can be taken out at any time should be enough to cheer you up.

- You may have thrown out your tree, but you can still pile your ornaments on the couch and celebrate all over again with a Christmas Cushion!

- Do not read *The Road*.

- Many department stores have old men who will let you sit on their laps year-round. Best of all, it's free!

- Give yourself one more present by ordering a pizza, shaking the box next to your ear, and then opening it while sitting cross-legged on the floor.

- Why are you trying not to be depressed? Frankly, you're more enjoyable to be around when you're sad.

- Don't forget that no matter how fat you are now, at least one person in the world is fatter. Gross.

- Consider the number of shitty presents you received. Remind yourself you don't give shitty presents. Now, pat yourself on your superior back!

- Every office has that one person whom nothing seems to get to. Punch that person in the face.

- Compared to your everyday blahs, the post-holiday blahs may not be that bad.

- Induce coma and get woken up on Mar. 20.

New Year's Resolutions

Every year, Americans celebrate the New Year by resolving to change some aspect of their lives. What's *your* resolution?

Darcy Fletcher
Elevator Inspector

"Thanks for the heads-up. I'm going to make my resolution now and get a week's jump on all the other chumps."

Ross Bernstein
Systems Analyst

"I observe the *Jewish* New Year, Rosh Hashanah, which has already happened. For that New Year, I resolved to let everyone know that January 1st is not the only New Year."

Matt Tulley
Cabinetmaker

"I'm glad New Year's is coming up. I've been looking for an excuse to finally take care of this gangrenous leg."

Accountants Pack Times Square For Fiscal New Year

NEW YORK—Amidst a blizzard of white, yellow, and pink forms in triplicate, a jubilant crowd of more than 800,000 accountants jammed Times Square Saturday night to ring in the fiscal new year.

The Fiscal Ball drops, ushering in the new year.

"Fiscal Year 2001–02!" shouted one unidentified CPA, a tie wrapped around his forehead and a paper-bag-covered bottle of caffeine-free Diet Coke in his hand. "The expense-accrual forms are completed and the statutory salary recovery requests are in. Now it's time to par-tay!"

The man then climbed atop a garbage can and wildly waved a copy of a PricewaterhouseCoopers end-of-year report before falling back into the crowd.

"Oh, yeah!" yelled 49-year-old Deloitte & Touche accountant David Gelfand, tear-ing off his shirt to reveal the phrase "In The Black" painted on his chest. "Anyone looking for final approval for payment vouchers subject to post-payment audit can forget it. The Office of Accounting is officially closed for the year! Whoooooo!"

Many present for the annual Times Square mayhem wore hats and carried noisemakers, and floating through the air were thousands of balloons emblazoned with the logo of the Big Five accounting firm Ernst & Young, the event's official sponsor.

Accountants began to gather as early as noon in anticipation of the official countdown to midnight, April 15. At first, the mood was calm and genial, with accountants discussing tax code and sharing their Fiscal New Year's resolutions with one another. But as day turned to night, the scene changed, with celebrants yelling, climbing onto parked cars, and throwing items from

> ### "'Oh, yeah!,' yelled 49-year-old Deloitte & Touche accountant David Gelfand, tearing off his shirt to reveal the phrase 'In The Black' painted on his chest."

their briefcases, including pocket calculators, spill-proof coffee mugs, and Parker pen sets. By 9 p.m., the size of the roiling throng had forced police to close off Broadway from 34th Street to 57th Street and re-route all vehicular traffic.

Shortly after 10 p.m., a portion of the crowd began to chant, "Excel! Excel!" in unison, prompting another group to defend its preferred spreadsheet software with shouts of, "Lotus 123! Lotus 123!" As the two sides' intensity increased, the impassioned yelling turned to shoving, and police had to escort several accountants out of the crowd.

Throughout the evening, the Times Square Jumbotron showed clips of accounting highlights from FY 2000–01, as well as reflections on the past fiscal year by celebrities such as Gerard Truman, author of *The Truman Formula For Estimating Loss Leader Profitability Returns.*

"There's no question that 2000–01 was one incredible fiscal year," said Truman, his words echoing through Times Square. "Microsoft released Windows 2000, everyone changed their methods to accommodate the Euro, and Office Max released its biggest catalog ever. But now, after a long, hard year of accounting, it's time to turn off our NQS batch queues and just enjoy ourselves."

One minute before midnight, the traditional countdown began as the three-ton, Tiffany-made Fiscal Ball slowly descended from the sky at One Times Square.

"That Fiscal Ball is the most beautiful thing I've ever seen," said Peter Timmins, 38, a KPMG budget analyst from Philadelphia. "Back when I was getting my master's in accounting at Georgetown, we'd all sit glued to the live annual broadcast of *John Kenneth Galbraith's Fiscal New Year's Rockin' Eve.* And now I'm actually experiencing it in person."

Lou Dobbs, former star of CNN's Moneyline, officially closed the ceremonies, addressing the crowd from atop a giant adding machine shooting reams of number-filled streamers into the crowd below.

"Let us now, for but a moment," Dobbs said, "look back fondly on FY 2000–01—the mergers and acquisitions that made it special, the new information systems that came into our lives, the new tax strategies we may have discovered in places we weren't even looking."

> ## "Shortly after 10 p.m., a portion of the crowd began to chant, 'Excel! Excel!' in unison, prompting another group to defend its preferred spreadsheet software with shouts of 'Lotus 123! Lotus 123!'"

Dobbs paused shortly, waiting for the crowd to quiet, before bursting into song.

"Should auld accountants be forgot..." sang Dobbs, lifting his voice as the swaying crowd of accountants linked arms and joined him in song.

"This is so amazing," said Amanda Lakewood, a tax-code accountant who traveled all the way from Merced, CA, to be part of the Times Square festivities. "When we're all here together, it doesn't matter if you work in budget analysis, auditing, or management accounting. It doesn't matter if you work for the government, a privately held corporation, or a public accounting firm. When we're together here like this, we're all just accountants, every one of us. Happy Fiscal New Year!" ∅

Leftover Christmas Billboard Stirs Seasonally Inappropriate Emotion

ST. LOUIS—Local architect Steve Burillo felt a momentary flush of seasonally incongruous holiday spirit Tuesday when he saw a Christmas-themed billboard on South Broadway. "The sign was advertising the St. Louis Ballet's performance of *The Nutcracker*, and for a second, I felt a stirring desire to volunteer for a charity and spread goodwill amongst my fellow men," Burillo said warmly. "But then I was like, 'Screw it. It's March. I should get to the gym and get in shape for summer.'" Burillo added that they really ought to take the billboard down before someone goes out and spends quality time with loved ones.

Child Bored With Christmas Puppy

HAMILTON, OH—Household sources reported Monday that Joshua Hunt, 10, has lost interest in Raggles, the 4-month-old cocker spaniel he received on Christmas Day. "For the first month, he played with it every day," said Joshua's mother Kathie Hunt. "Now he plays Nintendo as soon as he gets home from school and tells Raggles to shut up when he barks." Joshua has asked his mother if he can exchange the puppy for *Mario Kart 64*.